The Films of Shirley MacLaine

The Films of Shirley MacLaine

Patricia Erens

South Brunswick and New York: A. S. Barnes and Company
London: Thomas Yoseloff Ltd

© 1978 by A. S. Barnes and Co., Inc.

A. S. Barnes and Co., Inc.
Cranbury, New Jersey 08512

Thomas Yoseloff Ltd
Magdalen House
136-148 Tooley Street
London SE1 2TT, England

Library of Congress Cataloging in Publication Data

Erens, Patricia, 1938–
    The films of Shirley Maclaine.

    Filmography: p.
    Bibliography: p.
    Includes index.
    1. Maclaine, Shirley, 1934–   I. Title.
PN2287.M18E7   791.43'028'0924 [B]   76-50188
ISBN 0-498-01993-4

To my children
    Bradley and Pamela . . . two shining stars

Contents

Foreword, by Edith Head

I've worked with practically every star in the motion picture industry and, as a rule, they fall into definite categories. However, Shirley MacLaine is the exception. She is a complete individualist and the versatility she displays in her films is actually almost a carbon copy of her own personality. Shirley is a little bit like a chameleon. She changes constantly, and while she is never temperamental, there is always the element of excitement and the unexpected in working with her.

I find that this book translates very well the MacLaine mystique, and it, too, has the charm and versatility of Shirley herself. I truly enjoyed reading the book because it really tells the Shirley MacLaine story.

Edith Head

Edith Head

Acknowledgments

I would like to thank the following people who were kind enough to share information with me on Shirley MacLaine: Mary Day, Bob Fosse, Pete Hamill, Jack Lemmon, Zita Rudolph, and Claudia Weill. Also, I am grateful to Douglas Lemza of Films Incorporated, Patrick Sheehan of the Library of Congress Motion Picture Section, and Earl Warren of CBS-TV for the opportunities they provided to screen the necessary films.

Among the other people and organizations who gave me help and information are ABC-TV, Jonas Halpern (Rogers & Cowan, Inc.,), W.W. Norton & Company, David Parker (Library of Congress Motion Picture Section), Anthony Slide (The Academy of Motion Picture Arts and Sciences), and Jackie Thomas (Independent Television Corporation — England).

Most especially I am endebted to Luz Campos, who worked diligently on the preparation of the manuscript, to Stuart M. Kaminsky, who read the first draft and offered suggestions, and to Helen Fadim, who spent considerable hours editing the final version.

For photographs, credit goes to Cinemabilia, Claudia Weill (New Day Films), The Memory Shop, Movie Star News, and Time, Inc.

Lastly, I am most grateful for the help and support of my publisher, Julien Yoseloff and editor, Thomas Good, who aided me every step along the way.

Introduction: The MacLaine Image

From the moment that Shirley MacLaine landed in Hollywood, it was apparent to all observers that someone really fresh had arrived—a true original. What critics sensed emanated from MacLaine's perky, uninhibited screen portrayal in Alfred Hitchcock's *The Trouble with Harry,* as well as her direct, unaffected off-screen personality. In combination, one image reinforced the other, creating a distinctly new kind of star: on screen a more down-to-earth woman than American audiences were accustomed to in the midfifties; offscreen an actress who shunned the usual glamorous life associated with Hollywood celebrities.

Her screen test, now legendary in the annals of film history, was a preview of things to come. Perched on a high stool, MacLaine simply answered questions posed by director Daniel Mann from behind the camera. After casually holding forth about her life and ideas, she performed several numbers from *The Pajama Game,* a Broadway show in which she was appearing as Carol Haney's understudy. Her ease in front of the camera, coupled with a disarming, personal candor and obvious musical talents, impressed even the jaded Paramount staff who had seen many a starlet come and go. MacLaine's droll wit and extraordinarily expressive face were spontaneous. On camera she seemed totally un-self-conscious, her performance flowing naturally, effortlessly.

In contrast to the dominant female images of the fifties, MacLaine possessed neither the sensuous softness of Marilyn Monroe, nor the sultry sophistication of Elizabeth Taylor. Neither did she demonstrate the cool aristocratic bearing of a Grace Kelly or an Audrey Hepburn; rather, MacLaine represented a real woman, one whose responses were more in touch with the millions of moviegoers. Combined with high energy, optimism, and a tinge of the tomboy, she reminded many of the characters played by Debbie Reynolds and Doris Day. Yet film critic Molly Haskell has pointed out:

> Day and Reynolds represented not just naturalness, but naturalness as a convention, as a reaction to something else, the way producers of commercials use nonactors, "real" housewives and balding men, to counter the hype and falsehood of the message itself.[1]

Reynolds' bubbly personality and Day's enterprising efficiency bespoke of sunny days and ultimate triumphs, whereas MacLaine (especially in the roles of whores and waifs) masked loneliness and heartache behind her devil-may-care antics. Less intelligent and self-assured, MacLaine managed to muddle through, often suffering the scars of life's battle along the way. Neither servicing men's desires like Monroe nor denying her own sexual urges like Reynolds and Day, MacLaine revealed a human vulnerability nurtured by a need to be loved.

From the first, MacLaine rebelled against the star image in her private life. Dressing in comfortable, loose-fitting, old clothes, driving a second-hand Buick, appearing with uncombed hair, and living in an unpretentious beach house in Malibu, she continued to live her life as she had always done, uninfluenced by studio dictates, performer competition, and audience expectations. As she said later, "Being an actress is what I do; not what I am." What began as an anti-Hollywood gesture against the commercialization of performers eventually blossomed into a rejection of many long accepted middle-class values. MacLaine refused to be treated as an object or commodity and equally resisted the pressures to conform and be respectable. In 1956 she and her husband, actor-director-producer Steve Parker, set up separate households, circumventing the established tradition of "togetherness" in marriage. Prompted by the necessities of their separate careers Parker went to Japan to promote lavish theatrical productions throughout the Orient, while MacLaine chose to continue her acting career in Hollywood. Neither partner chose to dominate the other or to submerge individual creative talent in the success of the other. Suddenly, air fares and long-distance telephone calls became an expensive item in the budget. Onlookers were puzzled by an unusual marriage arrangement in a milieu noted for unusual marriage arrangements. Yet despite suspicions of marital discord and forecasts for an early demise, the Parker marriage held for almost fifteen years. Based on concepts of independence and mutual respect, their relationship was a model "open marriage" and went a long way in redefining the roles of men and women for the pre-1960 generation.

Obviously the unconventionality of MacLaine's offscreen life affected her onscreen images, even in the many formula films provided for her by Hal Wallis, with whom she had a five-year contract. Reporters labeled her a "kook," an "odd-ball," even "screwed-up." Audiences responded to her screen persona, mixing fact with fiction. Directors like Alfred Hitchcock, Vincente Minnelli, and Billy Wilder all sensed an ebullient versatility as each in turn focused on a different aspect of her emotional range. In *The Trouble with Harry* (1955), MacLaine's first film, Hitchcock captured a whimsy and feyness perfectly in tune with his own offbeat sense of humor. In *Some Came Running* (1958), the film that established her as a star (and produced the first of three Academy Award nominations), Minnelli concentrated on her open-

ness and defenselessness, which made MacLaine's portrayal of the guileless Ginny both sympathetic and believable. Despite Ginny's willingness to be used by men, her genuine compassion and enthusiasm saved the role from a sexist treatment of "woman as tramp." Ginny became the prototype for future roles as the happy and not-so-happy hooker with a heart of gold, which MacLaine played until 1968, culminating in her interpretation of *Sweet Charity*. Unlike the tarts and hussies that have graced the screen in the past, however, MacLaine women-of-the-streets were not especially sexy. As she herself commented, "You can't make cheese out of chalk." Often, as with Ginny, these women were more childlike than churlish, carrying stuffed animal purses or wearing ribbons in their hair.

MacLaine's performances in *The Apartment* (1960) and *Irma la Douce* (1963), both directed by Billy Wilder, were two of the best of her career. As Fran Kubelik *(The Apartment)*, the part-time mistress of a gadabout married executive, MacLaine once again demonstrated the good-natured naïvete that had typified Ginny. But in contrast to the lower-class prostitute in *Some Came Running*, Fran was a middle-class office worker, not so different from many females who sat on the far side of the screen. The film was one of the first movies of the decade to demonstrate that blond, buxom broads did not have a monopoly on sex and that premarital affairs were neither glamorous nor obscene.

In *Irma la Douce* (1963), Wilder tapped the brassy side of MacLaine's personality, exposing her self-assurance and ingenuity. Revealing a natural tendency towards comedy, which caused the late producer Mack Sennett to call her the greatest comedienne since Mabel Normand, MacLaine played the *poule* Irma, a professional woman in every sense of the word. Once again MacLaine established her own moral code and proved that whores were not necessarily tough cookies but, like other women, were capable of loyalty and affection. Played for laughs, the film nonetheless contained Wilder's cynical view of society's mores and hypocrisy, thinly disguised behind witty barbs.

Onscreen MacLaine perfected the role of the affable mistress or down-trodden prostitute who was short on brains but long on common sense. Offscreen she proved herself an independent, intelligent woman. Driven by an insatiable curiosity about how others live, she traveled thousands of miles, visiting every continent, seeking out inaccessible regions of Africa and India. Unsatisfied with a tourist's bird's-eye view, she lived among .the primitive Masai in the hinterlands of Kenya and with the ascetic Bhutan in their mountain kingdom in the Himalayas. Enduring drinks made of milk and blood, houses built of mud and dung, incredible filth, icy altitudes, and an attack of cholera, MacLaine learned that humanity is various indeed.

In 1972 she was one of the first Westerners to visit mainland China. As the invited guest of the Chinese People's Republic, she led the first women's delegation on a trip covering twenty-four-thousand miles.

Traveling was always a way of life, to be worked in and around her career. MacLaine's involvement in politics, however, was slightly different. She had always supported liberal causes. To many she became known as "a bleeder." When her career began to slide downward in the middle sixties, she searched for more meaningful commitments. She protested against the execution of Caryl Chessman and traveled throughout Mississippi in support of the civil rights movement. In 1968 she attended

the Chicago Democratic Convention as a delegate from California. It was in Chicago that MacLaine first became attracted to the youthful Senator George McGovern, whose enthusiasm and idealism promised a better, more open society. When she decided to support the candidacy of McGovern for president, MacLaine took on a full-time job. Abandoning her career entirely, she devoted her full energies from February to November 1972 to campaigning for his election throughout America. MacLaine was energetic and informed, not just a decorative star attraction who made occasional personal appearances. She assumed office duties, slept in small-town motels, and shook hands for hours on end.

By the early seventies MacLaine had come to represent the "new woman" in the minds of many American women. Self-educated, self-opinionated, and self-propelled, MacLaine became a model, not just of the successful woman who had made it in a man's world, but of a woman who had gotten there on her own terms. Without the loss of femininity, she created her own image, ignoring the ready molds that women had conformed to for so long.

How does such an image tally with her film roles as "happy hooker" and "husband hunter?" How could so intelligent a star play so many dumb dames? The answer lies in MacLaine's special approach to her roles. Despite the stereotypical characters meted out by the story department, MacLaine has always managed to inject a strong dose of her own personality into her parts. Most particularly, her straightforward naturalness often violates convention and has saved many roles from becoming mere caricatures.

Two aspects of her screen personality were responsible for her unique persona, indicating even in the early films a new conception of women's roles. One was MacLaine's attitude towards sex; the other, her offbeat, somewhat maverick code of conduct. Both characteristics broke new ground, providing an opportunity to make statements about women's sexual drives, the hypocrisy of the double standard, the need to discard outmoded social conventions, and the importance of defining one's self-image.

Although regulations concerning the subject of sex on the screen had been challenged by Otto Preminger as early as 1953 in *The Moon is Blue* (which was released without a seal of approval), the relaxation of the Production Code (fondly known as the Breen Code) did not actually take effect until the early sixties. Reacting to a host of European films that invaded America in 1959 (*The Lovers, Room at the Top, Hiroshima, Mon Amour,* and *Lady Chatterly's Lover*), Hollywood producers began to search for adult themes that portrayed sex in a more realistic manner.

As Molly Haskell has pointed out, the films of the fifties "were all about sex, but without sex." While most Hollywood films continued to label women as bad or good girls (*Baby Doll, Peyton Place,* and *Cat on a Hot Tin Roof* vs. *High Society, Pillow Talk,* and *Tammy*), MacLaine created a series of roles that were not so easily categorized. Unlike Doris Day characters who were always protecting their virginity, or Debbie Reynolds heroines who seemed to have no urges to protect, MacLaine women reached out for love without the illusions of romance. From 1959 to 1963, MacLaine starred in *The Apartment, The Children's Hour, Two for the Seesaw,* and *Irma la Douce*—each of which made a significant statement about women's sexuality.

In *The Apartment* (1960), MacLaine as the spirited, gullible Fran slept with Fred MacMurray because she loved him. The film implied that if Fran ended up in the lurch it was not because she was immoral — rather, that she had not realized she was a person. Her constant tendency toward self-depreciation (a trait that appears in many MacLaine vehicles) simply emphasized her lack of self-identity. In a subtle way it dramatized the necessity of developing a feminine consciousness. Although the film closed with the ubiquitous happy ending (Jack Lemmon's proposal of marriage), audiences were not indifferent to the lesson to be learned from Fran's situation.

In 1962, MacLaine again broached a new subject as a latent homosexual school teacher in William Wyler's *The Children's Hour.* Although the film seemed mainly concerned with portraying the destructive effect of vicious rumors on the lives of MacLaine and Audrey Hepburn, the movie did establish a precedent, opening the way for more detailed treatments of the subject later in the decade. *The Children's Hour* did not acknowledge that sexual feelings between two women could be happy, even normal, but it at least suggested that two women could build a life together without men and marriage.

Two For the Seesaw made in 1962 went even

further in portraying the plight of the average single girl. Despite Gittel Mosca's Bohemian trappings, her life wasn't terribly different from that of many women over twenty who were lonely and unmarried. Playing down the New York mannerisms that characterized the stage version, MacLaine spoke to a broader segment of the female population. Again she showed that living with a man wasn't particularly illicit or even sophisticated. That she got dumped in the end was a result of the particular men she chose to sleep with, not the result of breaking the existing moral code.

With *Irma la Douce* (1963), MacLaine finally cast off the image of the insecure, ill-used ingenue, blossoming into a strong-willed, self-determined woman. Gathering steam from her earlier roles in *The Matchmaker* (1958) and *Can-Can* (1960), she broke all the rules and came out on top. Demonstrating that there's a difference between professional prostitution and sexual love, Irma was able to keep each life separate. Although she serviced men for an appropriate fee, her occupation did not warp her emotionally or affect her self-image. Like other professionals, she prided herself on a job well done, and such acts never diminished her personally. Positive about her sexuality, Irma generated vibrancy.

More recently, MacLaine made the definitive, if slightly ironic, comment on women's sexuality. Reversing the gender of the classic *The Captain's Paradise,* a British comedy that depicted the pleasures of a wife in every port, MacLaine portrayed the glorious possibilities of having both husband and lover under one roof in *The Bliss of Mrs. Blossom.* Although the mannered style implied that such a life was not everyone's cup of tea, MacLaine's fantasies were no more than Technicolored vignettes of ordinary female daydreams.

As the MacLaine characters presaged a coming sexual freedom, her offbeat behavior was a fresh breath of air that spoke of individuality. In retrospect, much of what critics and writers referred to as "kooky" or "odd-ball" now seems rather conventional. The casual clothes, sensible hair styles, plain language — both onscreen and off — have become part of life in the sixties and seventies. More importantly, the directness and honesty of MacLaine's comments, her willingness to point to "the Emperor's nudity," are now regarded as a sign of integrity, not stupidity. In an age so filled with shams and duplicity, MacLaine's frank responses were a welcome antidote. It is clear now that the oft-repeated epithets simply meant that MacLaine was a decade ahead of the times.

From the perspective of 1975 many of MacLaine's early films take on a new meaning. What appeared innocent in films like *Ask Any Girl* (1959), *Can-Can, The Apartment, Two For the Seesaw,* and even *Some Came Running* now seems to provide important insights. In an age that values challenge over slavish acceptance, the MacLaine characters seem the smartest of all. Choosing individuality over conformity, naturalness over artificiality, and genuine love over social advancement, her heroines instinctively opted for the right values.

Like most studio stars, not all of MacLaine's pictures were memorable. Along with the challenging films, she also appeared in many forgettable films — especially between 1963 and 1968. Generally the fault lay with the script and the direction, as MacLaine's performances usually drew favorable reviews. Some critics, however, did note her tendency to rely on tried and true characterizations and wearied of the familiar mannerisms such as her high-pitched giggle, crinkly smile, raised eyebrows, cocked head, and quizzical face. But even in the nonsense comedies like *What a Way to Go* (1964), *John Goldfarb, Please Come Home* (1964), and *Gambit* (1966), MacLaine's portrayals touched on the situation of woman, what she was, who she was, and what she could become.

Most importantly, the films exposed the false dichotomy that had always existed between what male society expected and envisioned woman to be and what she really was. In film after film MacLaine played a dual role, reflecting the split personality of American females — a split accentuated by the repressive Eisenhower Era. It was a period in American history that still paid homage to the double standard.

The dual aspect of MacLaine's personality took various forms. Sometimes, as in *The Sheepman* (1958), it reflected the ease with which women, especially in the more flexible frontier societies, could move between traditional male and female roles. As Del Patton, MacLaine seems equally comfortable donned in pants as an outspoken horsewoman as she does as the ladylike hostess decked in frilly skirts for the local dance.

But in most roles the split occurs between the false and the true image. The false image is characterized by contrived behavior and an artificial appearance. In place of the spontaneous and candid, the false image elevates the premeditated and devious; in place of naturalness it fosters affectations. In some films the difference between the two roles is not very great — hardly more than a change of clothes. The clothes, however, are often an indication of what lies beneath.

Without exception, the false images are imposed by men or are initiated in an effort to gain male acceptance. In both *Two For the Seesaw* and *Sweet Charity,* MacLaine's lovers seek to play Pygmalion to her willing Galatea. In both cases the efforts are for nought. Despite the efforts of Robert Mitchum and John McMartin to upgrade MacLaine, she remains true to herself, resulting in both cases in the loss of the lover. However, the failure to be accepted for herself in these films is compensated for in *Can-Can, Ask Any Girl,* or *All in a Night's Work* in which MacLaine effects a change in her mate.

The dichotomy between the two images becomes more obvious in those films where MacLaine actually uses disguises to separate the two roles. Whether adopted by choice as in *My Geisha,* or at the instigation of a man as in *Ask Any Girl* and *Gambit,* the disguise is always used in the service of pleasing a male character, becoming the kind of woman he wants. There is even a short episode in *Can-Can* where MacLaine attempts to imitate the ladylike manners appropriate to the upper classes in an effort to impress Louis Jourdan. MacLaine's double roles thus emphasize the gap between the male-female view of womanhood. The false MacLaine wears seductive clothing, heavy makeup, elaborate hair styles, and uses ingratiating manners. In contrast, the true MacLaine wears sensible clothing and has a scrubbed face, simple hair styles, and independent opinions.

In addition, the false roles became a critique of the inadequacies of men's view of women. It is important that, at the end, the false image is always unmasked, revealing the true character beneath. In all instances the real MacLaine character emerges as superior, wiser, and more vital. Throughout the film the male characters are slowly prepared to recognize her real value; thus, the films become an educational process for the men, transforming the stuffy David Niven *(Ask Any*

Girl), the crusading Louis Jourdan *(Can-Can)*, and the priggish Cliff Robertson *(All in a Night's Work)* into more human, responsive adults. Likewise, her forthright approach to life is able to effect changes in scoundrels like Michael Caine *(Gambit)* and mashers like Dean Martin *(All in a Night's Work)*.

The use of disguises or alter-ego personalities as a means of achieving a goal (usually defined in terms of "getting a man," but not always) was not unique to MacLaine. Role-playing has long been associated with the female character. Molly Haskell states:

> In one sense, the actress merely extends the role-playing dimension of woman, emphasizing what she already is. By tradition, there were two occupations by which a woman "went professional," that is, got paid for doing what she already did: prostitution, in which she is remunerated for giving sexual pleasure, and acting, a variant on natural role-playing. A woman plays roles naturally in self-defense: As the sought-after rather than the seeker, she is placed on the defensive. She adopts masks and plays roles that will enable her to stall for time, stand back, watch, intuit, react. But she also plays roles, adapts to others, "aims to please," because of the central place of love in her life and the need to have her value confirmed by affection and attention.[2]

Haskell's quotation is especially appropriate to MacLaine, who utilized both forms of "professionalism" in her screen career: playing prostitutes in *Some Came Running*, *Irma la Douce*, *The Yellow Rolls-Royce*, *Two Mules for Sister Sara*, and *Sweet Charity;* and playing performers in *Can-Can*, *My Geisha*, *Two For the Seesaw*, *Gambit*, and *Sweet Charity*. Haskell's description applied loosely typifies all of MacLaine's roles.

Despite the obvious tendency to interpret MacLaine's split personality as a sickness of the times, her performances indicated signs of health on two levels. First, it is important to note that MacLaine's changes and disguises were always temporary, culminating in a return to her former self. It was as if play-acting gave her a chance to "try on" new images while she struggled to accept her self as she was. These disguises were always openly revealed, thus finally providing a clear delineation between the true and the false. Second, "the two faces of Eve" (sometimes more) indicated that just beneath the surface a fight was being waged. The double image was an outward symptom of the inward struggle for a new role. Although the constant play-acting seems to indi-

cate great ambiguity concerning the image of women, MacLaine's double roles were preferable to passive acceptance of ready-made stereotypes. There was promise that eventually women would emerge integral and whole, healthier than before, and shorn of the false attributes adopted at the instigation of men.

The logical extensions of MacLaine's dual roles were the two feature films in which she played multiple parts. Aside from the obvious appeal of such a *tour de force*, *What a Way to Go* and *Woman Times Seven* provided her with an opportunity to comment on the situation of women in various classes and differing societies. In particular, *Woman Times Seven*, composed of seven ironic vignettes, dramatized to what degree contemporary women continue to perpetuate rivalry, adopt false models, and hide behind self-delusions. None of the women are examples of liberated adults. All cling foolishly to retrogressive behavior patterns. Each fails to view herself and her situation objectively. Only the prostitutes in "Amateur Night" (the second vignette) offer a revolutionary, though perhaps unviable, response. However, the heroine is incapable of accepting such a solution. In the end, she rushes back into the waiting arms of her wayward husband and, like the other six heroines, sells out for a comfortable, self-defeating life.

It is only in MacLaine's most recent roles, in the films of the seventies, that her screen persona has synthesized into one consistent character. In *Desperate Characters* and especially in *The Turning Point*, films that have reaffirmed her ability as an actress, she has depicted mature, intelligent women who possess a sense of self-identity, although they may not have all of the ultimate answers.

Gone are the familiar mannerisms that identified her as an ingenuous imp. Partly it is that MacLaine has no doubt outgrown many of the obvious childlike attributes. But more relevant is that in the seventies it is now possible to be liberated in a quieter way. In the fifties and early sixties, for MacLaine's attitudes and behavior to have been acceptable to a large number of viewers, it was necessary for her to be slightly offbeat. Although she spoke for the hopes and wishes of many women who also wanted independence and the elimination of a double standard, not all were as willing to make themselves visible. While it was alright for "hookers," "kooks," and "odd-balls" to express their feelings and experience sex, it was not

yet respectable for others. In this way MacLaine suffered the bruises and spoke out for the voiceless majority. It was easy to sympathize with her since she was so clearly the underdog and since she seemed to pose no threat. In film after film she was outclassed by other characters and by us, the audience. Subtly, however, the point was made as MacLaine paved the way for changes for all women.

MacLaine's behavior no longer looks so avant-garde. The world has caught up with her and has adopted new values and new life-styles. At the same time, MacLaine no longer needs to play prostitutes or beatniks to enjoy freedom. In fact, her latest roles are all solidly middle class.

In recent years MacLaine has ventured into the male world of finance, turning her hand to both producing and directing. In 1971 she entered a partnership arrangement with Sir Lew Grade, Chief Executive of England's Independent Television Corporation. The contract specified a television series called *Shirley's World* and several pictures.

MacLaine's concept for the program was innovative. Anxious to portray a character similar to herself, she wanted to do something that would not be an insult to the American public.

> It would take place in the real world, and not in the vanilla ice-cream fantasy land where so many situation comedies took place. In fact, it shouldn't be a "situation comedy" at all. It could be a show that moved people, cheered them up, made them believe in the essential humanity of themselves and others. And it could mean something especially if it showed a woman doing more in her life than simply pampering a slow-witted husband, dealing with a mess of children, or accepting unhappiness with stoic good grace. I thought we could center it on a woman who was a professional reporter who wandered the four corners of the world without the protection of men, a woman who enjoyed her life and didn't have to call home for advice. I thought women would be able somehow to live vicariously through such a character, and that men would admire her and not be threatened by her.[3]

However, such noble ideas were not to be. There were script problems, producing problems, and problems with the crew. Rather than a portrait of the "new woman," the heroine of *Shirley's World* turned out to be a "nosy, irritating, empty-minded little banana head, who goes around the world bothering people."[4] Unable to exert sufficient control over the scripts, MacLaine was hardly surprised at the disastrous reviews.

Although producing has become a logical progression for Hollywood stars since the days Charlie Chaplin and Mary Pickford founded United Artists, directing has been an impossible dream for most. For women the opportunities were practically nonexistent. Since the arrival of sound in 1927, Ida Lupino and Elaine May have been the only actresses of note who directed themselves on the big screen.

Anxious to try her hand at so mysterious an endeavor, MacLaine decided to film her journey to China. Although this was hardly a big-budget Hollywood production, it did offer the opportunity to create and control her own vision. Four feminist filmmakers who had worked on independent film projects were invited to participate, and MacLaine and her crew recorded the unique, emotional experiences of the twelve women who ventured into a strange land. As producer, screenwriter, and co-director (along with Claudia Weill), MacLaine impressed her attitudes on the final presentation. After months of editing, superbly rendered by Weill (who was also responsible for the major portion of the camara work), *The Other Side of the Sky: A China Memoir* was shown on nationwide television in April 1975.

Not content with performing, producing and directing, campaigning and crusading, MacLaine also felt compelled to commit her life to print. In 1970 she published her autobiography, which quickly became the best-seller *Don't Fall Off the Mountain*. Covering her childhood, early successes, and life in Hollywood, the book ended with her return from India. In 1974, MacLaine wrote *You Can Get There From Here*, recording her experiences on television, the McGovern campaign, and her visit to China.

Now once again involved in filmmaking, she is hoping to produce and star in *Amelia*, the life of the world famous aviator, Amelia Earhart.

From floosies to fliers, it has been a long trip. To understand the transition, it is necessary to look more closely at the complete body of MacLaine's work, to see the development of the "new woman," especially to discover how she was imbedded in the old stereotypes. The following chapter outlines MacLaine's life and Hollywood career. The rest of the book is devoted to her films, the twenty-nine movies made between 1955 and 1977, and the documentary she herself directed in China.

The Films of Shirley MacLaine

1

Career: From Broadway to Hollywood—and Back Again

Shirley MacLaine, who came into this world as Shirley McLean Beaty, was born on 24 April 1934 in Richmond, Virginia. Her father, Ira O. Beaty, a well-educated real-estate agent who had once been a professional musician, ran the family with an iron hand. Her mother Kathlyn, a Canadian by birth, had done some acting and had taught college drama. Both were Baptist, solid citizens, and proud of their Southern heritage. In her autobiography, *Don't Fall Off The Mountain,* MacLaine refers to them as "a cliché-loving, middle-class Virginia family."

In looking back on her childhood, MacLaine recalls her close relationship with her brother Warren. Three years her junior, Warren, fondly called Little Henry by the adults, was truly a soul brother against the stifling conformity of small-town life. "Warren and I have been friends and allies since he was born. . . . I would have expired down there in Virginia if it hadn't been for him. But we both like to be King of the Mountain."[1] Together they feigned being model children and then secretly indulged in practical jokes and pranks behind their parents' backs.

No doubt a fortuitous confluence of ingredients worked to nurture the two future talents. A combination of native intelligence, boundless energy, and physical good looks prepared each to succeed in the years ahead.

From the earliest years, MacLaine was a tomboy. Although ballet lessons were begun at the age of three, such training did not feminize MacLaine, who could field a ball with the best guys and who often got into physical brawls protecting Warren.

At first, dancing lessons were not oriented towards a career; rather, they were considered a means of strengthening Shirley's weak ankles — a more pleasant pastime than other forms of therapy. However, dancing soon developed into a passion. Whether it was the free bodily movement or a love of being the center of attraction (pure exhibitionism), dancing quickly raced through Shirley's lifeblood.

When the Beaty family moved from Richmond to Arlington, Virginia, Shirley was sent to the finest dancing academy in the area: The Washington School of Ballet. Here teachers Lisa Gardiner and Mary Day groomed young girls and boys to take their places in the top ranks of America's best ballet companies. With stern discipline and infinite patience, these two women slowly molded tired bodies and unwilling muscles into strong, supple

had to go by the boards. Slowly, dancing began to consume Shirley's whole world. Life became a cycle of sweat and tears. However, it was not long before Shirley was admitted to the inner sanctum reserved only for those students who demonstrated a serious commitment to make dancing their life.

Miss Day, who remembers Shirley from the age of ten, claims that from the first she was outstanding, absolutely unique, even in the way she put things into words. Miss Day also recalls Shirley's sense of complete confidence, a trait that often marks those who succeed in the competitive world of the arts.

Twice a year The Washington School of Ballet staged public performances. At Easter the school performed a dance version of *Cinderella* and at Christmas a full-length ballet of *Hansel and Gretel.* Because of Shirley's height and a shortage of male students, she was always cast as a boy. When Shirley finally stopped growing, she reached a full 5'7" in her stocking feet. Five feet seven inches hardly seems unduly tall for a ballerina, considering the long, lithe bodies that form the backbone of a company like George Balanchine's *New York City Ballet.* But in the 1950s, Balanchine's preference for tall dancers was an exception, not the rule. Most companies still preferred shorter, petite physiques. When it became apparent to Shirley that she would have to consider an alternative to becoming a ballerina, she took the decision hard. She recalls having cried her eyes out one night, but in the end her indomitable spirit took over. She vowed "to make the most of whatever equipment I had been born with, and part of that equipment was to dare. But mostly I didn't want to be a disappointment to myself."[2]

Perhaps things have a way of going right for the wrong reasons. Despite Shirley's single-minded desire to become a classical ballerina, she possessed other talents that were better suited for musical comedy. Her 5' 6" stature (she claims to have shrunk one inch) with measurements of 34-24-34 was a considered ideal everywhere except on the ballet stage. In fact, *Photoplay* later called it the most perfect figure in Hollywood. Her bright red hair and freckles did not quite resemble an ethereal sylph, but it did animate her face and always drew attention from spectators when she appeared on stage. Most importantly, Shirley's comic bent made her a natural for the musical stage where she could freely express her feelings.

shapes. Carrying forward the great tradition of ballet masters of the past, Misses Gardiner and Day were sparse in their compliments. Not infrequently a young dancer would rush out of the practice room on the verge of tears, red with humiliation.

Yet, despite the exhausting physical demands and sober atmosphere, Shirley survived and blossomed. Her unshakable self-confidence and native good humor countered the stern formality of the world of ballet. Once- and twice-a-week lessons soon stretched into five days a week, with added rehearsals at night and on the weekends. School work was completed on the bus back and forth to ballet lessons; cheerleading and school activities

The talent for comedy showed up early in MacLaine's life:

At the age of four, she made her first public appearance — in a dancing school recital. As she made her entrance, she tripped and fell. Nothing she did for the rest of the evening got her quite as much applause.[3] That's when she got her first laugh and she's been an inveterate ham ever since.

Her comic forté showed up again when she was a chorus dancer in New York. While attending her roommate's wedding she claims:

I remember walkin' very slowly past that camera....I was so impressed by the wedding. It seemed beautiful to me. Everything was so tranquil and serious, and I was sure that some of my thoughts must have shown on my face....But Georgia showed the movie backstage at the theater one night, and when the film came to me, everybody laughed! It was a show that took me a long time to get over. I figured I was a clown, and no matter how hard I tried, I'd always be a clown.[4]

Taking herself in hand, MacLaine determined to have a career on the stage—whether it be ballet or not. During the summer following her junior year in high school she went to New York to dance in the chorus of a revival of Rodgers and Hammerstein's *Oklahoma*. MacLaine had spent the summers in New York since the age of fourteen. There she would take dance lessons all day and then collapse in bed at night, exhausted from the summer heat and long hours at the ballet barre.

When *Oklahoma* closed, the whole troupe was invited to perform at the Berlin Arts Festival. MacLaine carefully weighed the decision. Tempting as the offer was and anxious as she was to get her career under way, she finally decided to go back to Washington-Lee High School and finish her senior year. As she reasoned, there were many years ahead to build success, but this was the last chance to get her high-school diploma. She knew that once she left school, she would never go back.

Once graduated, MacLaine lost no time beating a trail to New York. Eighteen, wide-eyed, and full of ambition, she headed for the land of opportunity, waiting to be discovered. Her first apartment was at 116th and Broadway, near Columbia University — a fifth-floor walkup that featured low rent and low life. Later she lived on 73rd street. Meals consisted of peanut butter sandwiches and makeshift lemonade (water, ice, and free lemon slices meant to accompany iced tea) at the local Horn and Hardart Automat.

With the other young hopefuls, MacLaine trotted from audition to dance class and back again. Along the way she changed her name from Shirley Beaty (which was sometimes pronounced Beat-ee and other times Bait-ee) to Shirley MacLaine, a slight variation of her middle name. She landed a few chorus jobs in road companies and became a dancing decoration for a Servel Refrigerator trade show. After turning endless pirouettes in a white tu-tu, she showed up at one performance with blackened front teeth and was immediately fired. The manufacturer failed to respond to the quirky humor that was soon to make her into a star.

A former roommate of MacLaine's during the days of deprivation remembers that even offstage Shirley was a comic. "She always kept everyone in stitches — a million laughs." Her roommate also acknowledged that Shirley had a few unbeatable assets: beautiful red hair, blue eyes, a lovely complexion, and a great pair of legs. "You just couldn't miss her."

Back in New York, MacLaine joined the chorus of Rogers and Hammerstein's *Me and Juliet*. The year was 1952. Offstage she continued to live like a gypsy, eating whatever was cheapest and living in a walkup flat. The only changes in her life were chopping off her long red ponytail and her engagement to a graduate engineer. Although she had agreed to marry, his attitude towards her career (a passing fancy like a hobby) posed a perplexing problem.

Onto the scene came Steve Parker, part-time actor, part-time director, and would-be producer. "Right off, I didn't like him. He was good-looking, but he was too old. I was twenty and he was thirty-three. I was sippin' soda like I was still a high-school kid and he was guzzlin' beer like an old sailor. He was too sophisticated for me and he talked too much."[5]

Despite such initial reactions, the vibrations began, and the graduate engineer was quickly forgotten. MacLaine has commented that all of the positive events in her life have happened spontaneously. She is a firm believer in time, place, and circumstance.

In many ways MacLaine and Parker were an odd combination. He was cultivated, articulate, serious, and well traveled. She was provincial, earthy, and spontaneous. But in the end his sophistication matched her naiveté and they complemented one another. The two soon became an inseparable pair. In addition to their personal relationship, Parker also took on the job of theatrical coach. Later, after MacLaine got her big break, he became her personal manager.

In 1954, MacLaine moved from *Me and Juliet* to a new Broadway musical, *The Pajama Game*, directed by George Abbott and choreographed by Bob Fosse. In addition to dancing in the chorus, MacLaine had a small speaking part and doubled as understudy for star performer Carol Haney. Her pixie haircut made her ideal for the role. Bob Fosse, who later worked with her in *Sweet Charity*, remembered her at the time:

> A pleasant girl with red hair and freckles, very willing, with a kind of circus in her face. She had a piece of business, running out of a crowd and kissing the boss at a company party. It always got a roar. I thought, "Well, it's just a funny piece of business." Then she left for Hollywood, and they must have tried nine or ten girls doing this stupid thing, and it died. Then I realized Shirley had something special.[6]

MacLaine was warned that Haney was a healthy pro who never missed a performance. Despite such predictions, she set about learning her role. A chorus member remembers how MacLaine would stand in the wings, committing to memory every step and mannerism that Haney used. She even took to watching Haney offstage to discover whatever secrets such observations might yield. With intensity and determination, MacLaine bided her time.

And then, in a scene right out of a Ruby Keeler-Busby Berkeley musical movie, Haney broke an ankle. (Perhaps there is some hidden destiny in that ankles should once again play such an important role in MacLaine's dancing career.) On the first matinee, MacLaine arrived at the theater to discover she "was on." Shaking with nervousness, she stepped before a disappointed audience who had paid to see Carol Haney, and danced her heart out. Praying not to drop the black bowler in the famous "Steam Heat" number, she gained confidence as the audience warmed up to her. Despite many mistakes, one followed by an unrestrained "oh shit," she was an unqualified success, thus creating a bit of show-business history that keeps young hopefuls hoping.

But one night's success doesn't mean automatic stardom. MacLaine realized that her performance needed work and honing. Immediately, she and Parker set about perfecting each routine, he acting as critic and coach. The work was worth the effort. The second evening's performance was attended by Hal Wallis, Hollywood producer of such films as *Little Caesar, Jezebel, Casablanca,* and Dean Martin-Jerry Lewis films. After the performance, Wallis came backstage, and before morning MacLaine was the proud owner of one Hollywood contract.

Unfortunately, MacLaine lived to regret what seemed at the time a magic piece of paper. Bound to Wallis by a typical five-year contract, which later turned her into what she called a "white slave" contract, MacLaine was to have Wallis as her lord and master for a good many years to come. For the time being, Haney returned to the show, MacLaine moved back into the chorus, and life returned to normal. No telephone calls from Wallis! No movie offers.

But MacLaine's life has a way of providing unending opportunities, and it wasn't long before opportunity knocked a second time. Two months after the opening of *The Pajama Game*, Haney was out again—this time with laryngitis. Again MacLaine replaced her, and again the audience held a special guest. Herbie Coleman, an assistant producer for Alfred Hitchcock, happened to catch the show. He believed that MacLaine was perfect for the offbeat heroine of a new film still in the process of being cast. Coleman recommended her to Hitchcock, who came himself to see the prospective star.

Meetings ensued, and shortly MacLaine found herself in the autumn beauty of Vermont, and a new bride to boot. During a one-day break following her last performance, 17 September 1954, she and Steve raced to City Hall and were married. Their honeymoon took place on the set of *The Trouble With Harry*.

On hearing the news of MacLaine's wedding, Hitchcock said, "Why the hell did she have to get married at this point in her career? She shouldn't let anything hold her back!"[7]

From the beginning, MacLaine eschewed the qualities of a movie queen. She mixed with the crew and gorged herself with food (a pastime she still cherishes), and absorbed everything she could about moviemaking. Apart from helpful criticism from Parker, she had never taken an acting lesson. When the cast moved to California to complete filming, MacLaine and Parker opted for a rented house in Malibu Beach, as far from the artificial glamor of Hollywood as possible. With what little money remained, they bought a used green 1949 Buick.

In Hollywood, Wallis immediately threw her into a Dean Martin-Jerry Lewis musical comedy, *Artists and Models,* which gave viewers an ample opportunity to see MacLaine's curvey legs as well as hear her untrained voice. Even before the release of *The Trouble With Harry* (which didn't appear until November 1955) and *Artists and Models* (which followed in December), the studio press agents began the big buildup, which MacLaine did everything to sabotage. It particularly confounded the PR men that she didn't seem to know how lucky she was to be there. Gossip columnists began reporting on her antics and irreverent comments, most of which were unprintable. She quickly established a reputation as a conspicuously non-consuming celebrity. Words like sassy, madcap, and offbeat attached themselves to her name. But regardless of what was said, word was out that a new talent had arrived. In the January issue of *Look,* MacLaine was chosen along with the young James Dean (appearing in his first starring role in *East of Eden*) and British singer Julie Andrews as the bright new stars to be discovered in 1955.

In July, *Cosmopolitan* picked "seven sex goddesses to follow." Pictured among bathing-suit-clad starlets like Kim Novak, Sheree North, and Anita Ekberg, MacLaine was dressed in a terry cloth robe that covered all but her knees. Among such sexy company, she shown with her own light.

Meanwhile, as MacLaine awaited the release of both films, she made several television appearances: one with comedian Bob Hope and one as a last-minute replacement for Betty Grable, who ironically injured her leg and couldn't appear. *The Trouble With Harry* proved to be one of Hitchcock's least successful films, but critics were not unmindful of the fresh new face with the casual air. MacLaine also won praise for her comic performance in *Artists and Models.* With two films under her belt, she was well on her way, if not yet a household name.

At this point, Parker began to get restless. Bursting with ideas and ambition of his own, he was not content to sit around and become Mr.

MacLaine. Most specifically, he wanted to return to Japan where he had spent his childhood and army service during World War II. He had dreams of producing theatrical performances that would travel all over the Orient. He felt that he knew Japan and that he was the man who could bring this about.

And so Parker took off for the East, leaving MacLaine alone in their house in Malibu. Thus began what for many years was a strange but successful marriage, with Parker in Japan producing extravaganzas and MacLaine in Hollywood making films. Marriage by long distance didn't mean no communication, however. Telephone calls were frequent across the seven-thousand miles, and MacLaine thought nothing of boarding an airplane for Tokyo on the spur of the moment to spend a long weekend with Steve.

Not long after Parker departed, MacLaine met entrepreneur Michael Todd. Determined to have a "campy princess" for his new star-studded production, *Around the World in 80 Days,* he sold MacLaine on the film, promising her a chance to shoot in Japan. This was MacLaine's first exposure to the charming land of the rising sun, and from 1955 on she remained a life-long Japanophile, even learning to speak a respectable Japanese. Shooting for *Around the World* gave MacLaine her first taste of the world beyond America. In part it may have been responsible for her passion for traveling.

After shooting concluded, MacLaine returned to Hollywood to await the results of the film and a yet-to-be-born baby girl. Stephanie Sachiko was born 1 September 1956. Sachiko means "happy child" in Japanese and was given to Stephanie in memory of a child Parker had adopted. Parker was a member of the first American troop that entered Hiroshima after the war. There he found and befriended a little orphan. As he didn't know her name, he had called her Sachiko because she was always smiling. He planned to bring Sachiko back to the States to live, but before all the arrangements were made she died of radiation poisoning. As Stephanie Sachiko Parker grew, she was alternately called Sachi and Steffie and learned to make her home in both the United States and Japan.

The results of *Around the World in 80 Days* were anything but encouraging. Although the film did land-office business, MacLaine came off looking like a Sari-clad hoyden. Partly the fault lay

LIFE

FLORIDA'S MAIL ORDER LAND RUSH

NEW LINCOLN FIND RECALLS DAYS
IN SPRINGFIELD WITH HIS NEIGHBORS

THE SAUCY MacLAINES:
SHIRLEY AND DAUGHTER

FEBRUARY 9, 1959 **25** CENTS

with Todd's choice in the first place. Accepting MacLaine as a Hindu princess, albeit a "campy Hindu princess," just took too much imagination. *Time* called it a "memorable bit of miscasting."

Meanwhile, MacLaine's career began to slip. In order to continue working, she made several television appearances with Dinah Shore, Steve Allen, and other NBC performers. Then in an effort to develop her acting ability and to impress Wallis, she took a lead in a touring company of *The Sleeping Prince*. The excellent reviews did the trick. She had worked hard to establish her career. Determined to remain afloat, she stated, "If and when I'm a star, I don't want to be a fad. I want to be someone who will last."[8]

Convinced that MacLaine had more potential than a mere showgirl decoration, Wallis cast her in a film version of *Hot Spell*. This was MacLaine's first serious dramatic role. Anxious to return to films after a two-year hiatus, she jumped at the chance to play the daughter to Shirley Booth's Alma Duval. Shooting began on 6 March 1957.

Meanwhile, MacLaine resumed life as a promising young actress. But even as her star rose, she kept her eye on reality. After finishing her sixth film, *The Matchmaker*, she told a reporter, "I don't know where I got the idea I could act in the first place. I liked doing the part in *The Matchmaker* mainly because I dig good food and the script called for it. In a restaurant scene we had pheasant for five days and wine for a week."[9] Although she continued to live off the beaten track at Malibu Beach with her infant Stephanie, she began to make the rounds of dinner parties that always made the morning columns. From time to time she would even take Steffie in a basket, which started rumors about her casual, if not irresponsible, attitude towards motherhood. MacLaine's response was that people should mind their own business.

But parties quickly wore thin, and MacLaine spent many weekends home alone, reading. Her verdict on Hollywood high life: "All those dinner parties—with the same cast (guests), same crew (servants), same orchestra, even the same dumb dinner."[10] A prolific reader, MacLaine spent hours curled up with a book. She devoured books like chocolate sundaes, always reading for information to satisfy her boundless curiosity.

Gossip was also rampant concerning her marriage to Parker. Unable to accept a married woman living alone in Hollywood, columnists implied everything from predictions of divorce to accusations of adultery. Mostly MacLaine just laughed it off, but from time to time she told a reporter exactly what she thought in language that was generally shocking.

At about this time the word "kooky" became a ubiquitous adjective every time MacLaine's name was mentioned. In a *Time* article in 1959, *kook* was defined as "meaning, roughly, screwball. Pronounced to rhyme not with book but with fluke."[11] But a friend said,

> She is the least kook I know. People just can't seem to understand that Shirley isn't interested in doing what's safe or what's approved just to be accepted.[12]

And MacLaine's reply: "If you don't take a chance on making a fool of yourself every once in a while, you're only half alive."

Hot Spell was the break MacLaine needed to put her career back on the road. That year she made three more pictures—*The Sheepman*, *The Matchmaker*, and *Some Came Running*. MacLaine has little admiration for the first two films, having stated in her autobiography that she went from "one insignificant picture to another"; but actually *The Sheepman* was a compact little Western, and *The Matchmaker* showed her off in one of the most charming of her early roles. Together these films earned her the Hollywood Foreign Press Award as the most versatile actress of 1958.

For MacLaine, however, this period was a low point in her personal and professional life. She recalled, "I knew that my life was badly out of balance." To overcome loneliness and despondency, she submerged herself in work and devoted her full emotional energies to raising Sachie.

The turning point came in 1958 when Vincente Minnelli offered her the role of Ginny in *Some Came Running*, a film that starred Frank Sinatra and Dean Martin. Minnelli had seen MacLaine on television and wanted her for the role. MacLaine knew it was the part she had been waiting for but was outraged that Wallis refused to allow her the $75,000 Metro-Goldwyn-Mayer was willing to pay, holding her instead to the $10,600 stipulated in her contract. In the end, she couldn't bear to pass up the role, and so she agreed to Wallis's terms.

Some Came Running changed MacLaine's life in

several ways. First, it spiraled her to stardom and gained her her first Academy Award nomination. Accordingly, her salary rose from $10,000 to $250,000—most of which went to Wallis. Second, it established her screen persona as the down-trodden, good-hearted, simple-minded hooker—a role she would play with great success in films like *Irma la Douce, Sweet Charity,* and several others. Lastly, it put her in contact with Frank Sinatra and a group of actors who surrounded him, known as The Clan or The Rat Pack. These were the first actors with whom MacLaine felt a true sense of camaraderie. The clan consisted of Dean Martin, Sammy Davis, Jr., Peter Lawford, Tony Curtis, Joey Bishop, and other fringe members. As the only female member, MacLaine served as the mascot of the group.

Although debates raged as to the reality of such a group and to its solidarity, MacLaine did establish a life-long friendship with these people. They appealed to her for the same reason she appealed to them. They were free-thinking, spontaneous performers who may have had their professional hangups, but who, on the whole, enjoyed an uninhibited good time. This meant drinking (beer), playing cards (gin rummy), telling jokes, and lots of laughter. Referring to MacLaine, Dean Martin told a *Time* reporter, "She's also a great audience. She loves to laugh. I'd be the biggest hit in the world if I only had 500 like her in every audience."[13]

Within this happy, unsophisticated group, MacLaine felt at home—no fancy clothes, no pretense, no serious concerns. Although the group seldom assembled *en masse,* individually the members kept in touch and always had a warm sense of regard for one another.

After the release of *Some Came Running,* MacLaine was inundated with a flood of offers. She said, "Suddenly I found that while once I could never find the right part, now I was right for every part."[14] For her role in *Ask Any Girl*—the film that succeeded *Some Came Running*—MacLaine received the British Film Academy Best Actress Award and an award at The Berlin Film Festival. Both *Life* and *Time* magazines featured MacLaine on their covers in 1959. *Time* chose MacLaine as the representative of the New Hollywood. Realizing that she had been picked as a star of promise not yet arrived, she asked with typical candor, "Can you ever get on the cover a second time?"[15]

In discussing the new female personalities, *Time* was quick to note that as opposed to earlier days when starlets rose to the top posing for cheesecake, MacLaine had done it on her own terms without studio-supervised romances, sexy publicity shots, or even a swimming pool.

In Japan, Parker was finding equal success in his career. His show *Holiday in Japan* had three touring companies in the United States, and he was in the process of developing *Philippine Festival* for export. By 1961, Parker had offices in Bangkok and Hong Kong, as well as in Tokyo. With success, the Parkers sold their beach house and bought a house in Encino, California, in the San Fernando Valley. Later MacLaine kept an apartment in New York City, as well as a place in London.

Rumors continued to circulate about the Parker marriage. Suzy of the *New York Mirror* wrote:

> Maybe screen smash Shirley MacLaine and her husband Steve Parker are getting along splendidly, but that's not what their set is saying. Steve's just spending too much time in the Orient, no matter how many good deeds he's doing to keep the home fires burning. And Shirley's making all the money for the family.[16]

MacLaine's response to such comments: "It works for us, so why can't everybody leave us alone?"

Following *Some Came Running,* MacLaine launched into a series of films that ranged from straight drama to musical comedy. This period culminated in her performance in Billy Wilder's *The Apartment,* which earned her The New York Film Critics' Award and her second Academy Award nomination. Suddenly she was a star. In the Box Office Popularity Poll for 1960, MacLaine placed number three, right behind Doris Day and Elizabeth Taylor. *Look* magazine picked MacLaine for a special feature called "Four For Posterity," which included Marilyn Monroe, Elizabeth Taylor, and Judy Garland.

In between films and trips to Japan, MacLaine visited the countries of the world. In 1961 she went to Spain; in 1962 to Romania and the Soviet Union. Russia turned out not to be a favorite place. MacLaine stated, "I was shocked at the lack of individual personality among the people." Home was everywhere and nowhere. Sachie was now living in Japan with her father. Next to traveling, reading remained a passion. It was as if she had organized her own university education. Since MacLaine only sleeps four or five hours a night, she

LIFE

With husband Steve Parker — New York, 1955.

claims, "I have a problem. I have all this energy to burn up every day." Filled with boundless vitality, limitless stamina, and endless curiosity, MacLaine took in everything life had to offer.

Though her career was growing by leaps and bounds with new challenges appearing in profusion, one problem continued to plague MacLaine: her contract with Hal Wallis. What had begun as a standard five-year contract now stretched into seven and then nine years because of suspensions and extensions. Each time MacLaine took a leave of absence to travel or to star in a film like Parker's production, *My Geisha,* she was docked by so many months.

Long-term contracts had bound film actors since the twenties. Movie queen Bette Davis was one of the first actresses to take a stand against such treatment, but as late as the sixties such practices were still common.

MacLaine's complaint was twofold. In part she was prompted by the economic limitations it put on her earnings. Although she received offers in the six-figure category, for the nine films she made under Wallis's auspices, she averaged a measly $15,800 per picture. But second, and more important, was the inability to control her own career and to choose those vehicles that appealed to her. MacLaine balked at the immorality of "owing another person." The final confrontation arose over Wallis's insistence that MacLaine star in a film that she felt was "totally offensive."

Never one to back away from a good fight, MacLaine decided to take the case to court. Specifically, she planned to sue under the California Labor Laws, which stipulated that a service contract could not be enforced beyond a seven-year period. The vibrations of such an action raced through Hollywood. Although the studios may have sided with Wallis against such an upstart as

In Madrid, Spain, 1961.

MacLaine, no one wanted to see the case go to court. They feared a ruling against the long-term contract which might have undermined the structure that sustained the star system. So, for the sum of $150,000, Wallis released MacLaine from her contract. Immediately her income soared into the seven-figure category. Obviously she saw no discrepancy between a high salary and a commitment to the simple life. Such inconsistencies in the MacLaine personality often caused people to question her genuine spontaneity and honesty. Many wondered if her simplicity and directness were just a calculated pose.

The early sixties was a high point in MacLaine's career. Working with some of the best directors in Hollywood, she made *The Children's Hour* with William Wyler, *Two For the Seesaw* (1962) with Robert Wise, and *Irma la Douce* with Billy Wilder.

All around, new opportunities and experiences were opening up. The Parkers decided to try a joint venture with MacLaine as star and Parker as producer. The result was *My Geisha* (1962), filmed in Japan. The film contained many autobiographical references and reflected the abiding love that still existed between the two. In interview after interview, MacLaine, like a school girl, talked of how she adored her husband and even admitted that she "looked up to him" as well. Earlier, the two had talked about a big family, three or four children, but that was never to be. Two years later, based on the success of their first film, the Parkers produced another movie together, *John Goldfarb, Please Come Home*. Unlike *My Geisha*, *John Goldfarb* received some of the worst press reviews in MacLaine's entire career.

During this period MacLaine gave support to several causes and established herself as one of the liberal members of the Hollywood set. In 1959 she gave a benefit for the Japanese victims of the typhoons that had struck Nagoya. Gathering together a close group of friends, she persuaded them to perform in Las Vegas for six-hundred guests, thus raising $30,000. Later, MacLaine gave support to two orphanages—one in Japan, the other in India. During the sixties she also began to confront the issue of civil liberties. Along with Marlon Brando and Steve Allen, she went to Sacramento to protest the execution of Caryl Chessman. During the height of the Civil Rights Movement, MacLaine spent time in Mississippi, learning about discrimination firsthand, not from the newspapers.

Meanwhile, Warren's career was beginning to blossom. After a one-year stint at Northwestern University in Evanston, Illinois, Warren left school to become an actor. His break came in 1961 when he won the male lead opposite Natalie Wood in Elia Kazan's *Splendor in the Grass*. During this period Warren tended to keep his distance, anxious to "make it" on his own, not as Shirley MacLaine's baby brother. However, MacLaine claims they never were not on speaking terms as the press reported. Recently MacLaine said,

I love Warren, I admire him and am amused by him. We are very fond of one another, but we both have a very healthy, competitive nature. We like to outdo each other. We've both done well in movies. We've both led honest, but unconventional lives. And we are both interested in politics. We would someday like to work together.[17]

MacLaine has also stated that she both admired and respected Warren for his roles in *Bonnie and Clyde* and *Shampoo*—films in which he had the courage to reveal a portion of his inner self, which most actors prefer to conceal.

During the middle sixties MacLaine continued her hectic schedule of filming and traveling. She visited Paris and East Africa. She reached out further to countries and cultures beyond her own sphere. In 1964 she went to India and the tiny mountain country of Bhutan; in 1966, to Thailand and Laos. She did not, however, accompany Mia Farrow or the Beatles to meditate with the Maharishi, as some reported in the press. Her disgust for the ugly American abroad compelled her to write one of her first published pieces, an article entitled "The Pretty American Abroad." Published in a holiday issue of *Carte Blanche*, MacLaine had harsh words for those travelers who sought cheap jade and fast clothes in preference to an opportunity to learn and understand.

As the sixties wore on and good roles for women, especially those over thirty, began to dwindle, MacLaine turned more and more to other activities. She had always cared more about the life that lay beyond the camera than the sphere of activity in front of it. Traveling had provided some answers. In 1968 she said, "We all need more succinct answers beyond credit cards and two cars in the driveway. Once you get to Asia and try to understand their ancient cultures, you don't find people trying to top each other, and themselves, in this terrible competition."[18]

In Madrid, Spain, 1961.

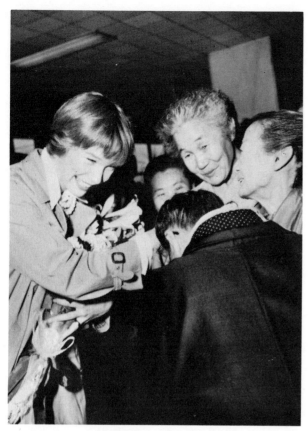

Arriving in Tokyo, 1958.

Increasingly, MacLaine turned to politics as a source of commitment and as a way of solving some of the ills she felt infected our society. She said, "Becoming committed is commensurate with maturity. I don't think of myself as an actress, as a movie star. I'm a person. I'm involved in society— American society. The basis of our democracy is individual commitment."[19]

In 1968, MacLaine campaigned for Robert Kennedy and was elected as a Democratic delegate to the convention held in Chicago. With the assassination of Kennedy, MacLaine shifted allegiance to McGovern. At the convention her presence was as prominent as Bella Abzug.

Following the convention, MacLaine began to appear in person and in print, forcefully expressing her ideas on every subject from nationalization to abortion. She was invited by the BBC to present an hour program on her view of American politics. MacLaine spoke out for the nationalization of all health services and the gas and oil industries. Basically she advocated a form of democratic socialism. In 1970 she became the first woman in 137 years to deliver a speech at the National

Democratic Club in New York. Here she urged men to consider sterilization in an effort to reduce overpopulation. In 1971 she was invited to address the Yale graduation class.

On several occasions, articles appeared announcing the possibility of MacLaine running for elective office. Once she was mentioned as a possible opponent to Senator George Murphy. Another time the newspapers stated that she had been asked to run as a Congresswoman from California but had turned it down. MacLaine herself stated that she had considered running as a Socialist in 1971 but had eventually abandoned the idea.

Unlike Jane Fonda, another prominent actress deeply involved in political agitation, MacLaine never alienated her public. Reflecting on this phenomenon, MacLaine stated recently, "For one thing, I've worked inside The Establishment, and always will. . . . And another thing is, I don't hate anybody."[20]

One issue that MacLaine has consistently fought for is the right of freedom of speech. In 1973 she fought proposed changes in the Federal Crime Statutes, which would classify certain films and books as obscene, thus making them unavailable to the public. In an article entitled "Eros and the Nixon Administration," published in *Newsweek,* she wrote: "For the first time in American history an Administration is attempting officially to legislate the morals of the public by imposing restrictions."[21] For MacLaine, this was an all-out political move to repress the creative arts. Later that year MacLaine resigned as a member of the American Film Institute over the issue of censorship. Again in 1976, MacLaine became a staunch supporter in Harry Reems's campaign to fight an obscenity charge growing out of his participation in *Deep Throat.*

By 1970, MacLaine's life had taken some major chances. Where once life consisted of a full-time film career and a part-time marriage, now life consisted of a part-time film career and a full-time life as a writer. Following the failure of an expensive *tour de force, Woman Times Seven,* and then the much anticipated *Sweet Charity,* MacLaine went into virtual retirement to try her hand at writing.

In a lively, honest, and highly humorous autobiography called *Don't Fall Off the Mountain,* MacLaine recounted her childhood in Virginia, her discovery in *The Pajama Game,* her rise to Hollywood fame, her marriage to Steve Parker, her irreverent attitude toward success, her world travels, and ultimately her inner sense of peace. The title of the book refers to Steve's cable, sent on the eve of her departure for Bhutan. It read: "GO BHUTAN AND LEARN. STOP. BUT DON'T FALL OFF MOUNTAIN."[22]

MacLaine claims to have been encouraged to write by William Lederer, author of *The Ugly American,* whom she had met in the Far East. Like most everything she does, she writes quickly and with great ease. She claims to have total recall of conversations, faces, and events. In addition to her natural wit, her writings also reflect insight gained through her exposure to psychoanalytic therapy.

Don't Fall Off the Mountain became an instant success and is perhaps one of the most intelligent, articulate autobiographies ever written by a movie star. It remained a best-seller for eight months, selling over eighty-thousand copies in hardcover. It still graces the racks of paperback bookstores where it has sold over one-million copies to date.

MacLaine's life was changing in other ways, too. Her long-term, long-distance marriage with Steve Parker was beginning to fray. Perhaps each had lived alone for too long; perhaps each had grown in different ways; or perhaps it was just that each had his own need to have a close relationship at hand.

Whichever, in 1968 MacLaine met Sander Vanocur, a successful, serious-minded television newsman. Vanocur had covered the Chicago Democratic Convention, which MacLaine had attended as a California delegate. At the time he was forty; she, thirty-three. During the following years the two were seen often in one another's company. Then in October 1970, an article appeared in *Photoplay* entitled: "Shirley MacLaine & Sander Vanocur: Free to Love or Free-Love?" This publicity was the beginning of a new chapter in the Parker marriage. Both announced that they had no intention of divorcing but agreed that each would chose to live his own life. MacLaine declared marriage obsolete and stated that there was no point in divorcing one man only to marry another. The Parker marriage made few headlines in the seventies, an era that witnessed every conceivable living arrangement. However, the honesty with which MacLaine conducted her affairs still proved a little avant-garde. Characteristic of MacLaine's forte for being slightly out-of-step, her new life was ultraliberal in a liberal age, as her previous life had

been too puritanic in a puritanic age. It was pure MacLaine.

Since 1970, Vanocur and MacLaine have gone their separate ways. Beginning in 1972 she shared an apartment with Pete Hamill, a journalist, novelist, and screenwriter. Like Vanocur, Hamill is intelligent and articulate. Describing life with Hamill, MacLaine states that he is steady, reasonable, solid, in contrast to her impulsive, blustery brashness. "What we've got is a combustible relationship. . . . We don't waste our time talking about marriage and the future and any of that crap.[23] Anyway, who knows? It could all be over next week."[24] Their relationship remained solid for over four years.

Following the success of *Don't Fall Off the Mountain,* MacLaine launched into a television series entitled *Shirley's World.* Produced by England's television entrepeneur, Sir Lew Grade (now Lord Grade), for American and British audiences, the show was planned to feature a roving news reporter, Shirley Logan, who traveled around the world gathering material. Sir Grade was anxious to gain a foothold in the United States and felt that an American star would turn the trick. For this venture he budgeted $20,000,000, the largest sum thus far spent on a British television series, and offered MacLaine a share of the proceeds. In addition to shooting twenty-four episodes, their deal called for two motion pictures, neither to exceed $3,000,000. Both *Desperate Characters* (1971) and *The Possession of Joel Delaney* (1972) were produced as part of this deal.

The show was fraught with problems from the beginning—all of which are elaborately recounted in MacLaine's second autobiography, *You Can Get There From Here,* published in 1975. The main fault seems to have been the inane scripts. As early as February 1971, MacLaine told Hollis Alpert in an interview for the *Saturday Review,* "I'm not too happy with some of them (scripts), particularly those that deal with the problems of areas I know. Because I've traveled so much, I'm extra sensitive to the cultural perceptions of those particular writers."[25] On the other hand, MacLaine had her own rather bizarre ideas about the program. She said, "I want to have the most fabulous-looking clothes and to wear the most unpredictable combinations. And a different hairstyle each week." There was also a great deal of resistance to MacLaine efforts to make Shirley Logan into a

Shirley's first television series: "Shirley's World."

liberated woman who held down a good job, got around on her own, and had more than one boyfriend to go to bed with.

Despite internal friction, in March 1971, MacLaine flew to London to begin work. Shooting took place in Hong Kong, Tokyo, and Nikko. Wherever possible, efforts were made to adapt the filming situation to capture the spontaneous events taking place around them.

The show previewed on 15 September 1972. The first episode centered around Shirley Logan's attempt to interview a British big wig who lived at a London Club restricted to men. To accomplish her goal, she politely blackmailed him with photographs. The high hopes for the show were soon dashed. Press response was wretched; the ratings terrible. MacLaine, who had gradually grown disillusioned about the project, felt vindicated, if not happy, about its failure. The show was cancelled after several episodes.

Exhausted and disappointed, MacLaine returned to America and threw herself into George McGovern's campaign for the presidency. Never afraid of a new challenge, she was also unafraid of changing priorities in midstream. As early as 1957, she reflected on the stagnation of many Hollywood stars:

> I feel sad sometimes for some of the great stars out here who can't seem to let go of what they've achieved. It's almost as if they're hopelessly stuck with it. Ambition's great—I have a good stack of it myself—but if I thought it was getting to be more than I could handle, I'd skedaddle for Vermont tomorrow.[26]

As if heeding her own advice, she sought a new way to utilize her talents and creativity. For eighteen months she lived the life of a politician, writing speeches, grabbing food on the run, shaking hands, and smiling.

MacLaine's special assignment was Chairman of the Women's Caucus. However, she put her talents to use in other ways as well, especially writing. For McGovern she wrote *The Man and His Beliefs*, which sold over one-hundred-thousand copies at a dollar a piece. On the campaign trail she spoke to women's groups, always composing her own speeches. Never one to mince words, she revealed a flare for writing and a comic touch that helped win friends for the cause.

Hollywood stars have long lent their support to political candidates, especially as fund-raisers and entertainers. But MacLaine's contribution was more than that of an attractive ornament. A member of McGovern's staff said, "What she does better than most people I've met in or out of politics is give people a sense of her own involvement with social change. And she has an access to McGovern that is deep and genuine. He listens to her."[27] One issue, however, on which McGovern did not listen was abortion. In the end MacLaine gave way, agreeing not to forward her personal views or say anything that would damage McGovern's chances of winning the election.

Indefatigable, MacLaine stayed with McGovern until the end, making impossible demands on herself, growing fat on junk food and seeing more of America than she dreamed existed.

During this period, she turned down several film offers. Later she regretted this decision. She was offered roles in *Forty Carats*, which later went to Liv Ullmann, and in *Pete 'n Tillie*, which eventually starred Carol Burnett. Also, for a while, she considered a film called *Long Division*, to be directed by Robert Altman, but the project came to naught. Over the years there were many roles that "got away" and several projects that never materialized. In 1959, MGM announced that MacLaine would star in her first singing and dancing role, *The Elsie Janis Story*, but the film never came to the screen. Earlier, MacLaine was cited as a lead in Frank Tashlin's *Hollywood or Bust*, but the part went to another. MacLaine even claims to have turned down the female lead in *Bonnie and Clyde*, opposite brother Warren, but states she would like to make a film with him some day.

Perhaps the two films that MacLaine regrets the most are *The Unsinkable Molly Brown* (1964) and *The Exorcist* (1973). MacLaine had made a deal with MGM to do *Molly Brown* at the height of her

dispute with Hal Wallis. MGM, running scared, withdrew the offer for fear Wallis would obtain a restraining order against her in the middle of production. The role then went to Debbie Reynolds.

The Exorcist was a different story. William Blatty had actually modeled the character of Chris MacNeil on MacLaine, a personal friend and neighbor in California. Blatty has written:

> I had always felt inadequate and insecure in my handling of female characterizations.... And so when starting the novel, I had looked about for a model for Chris MacNeil, one who lived in a milieu that I knew very well and who also had a mental set and personality that would make the story work: a flipness of manner (masking vulnerability) and an earthiness of tongue that would help to keep the situation rooted in reality.[28]

MacLaine liked the film and approached Lew Grade about financing. His enthusiasm was less, however, and his offer insufficient to please Blatty; thus, MacLaine missed starring in one of the biggest box-office hits of the decade.

By the time campaigning for McGovern ground to a deadly halt, MacLaine was asking some serious questions about America—about its values and its way of life. Despite the resounding defeat, MacLaine was not disillusioned. She commented that "McGovern was totally about change, and that scared the hell out of the public. Men like McGovern are necessary at times in history to let us know we are going too slow."[29] At this juncture in time, she was given a unique opportunity to test her principles and to accomplish an old, childhood dream. Through Chiao Kuan Hua, the Chinese foreign minister whom MacLaine met in New York in 1971, she was extended an invitation to visit mainland China.

The invitation eventually led to a three-week trip together with eleven other American women, four of them filmmakers. Representing a cross-section of the United States, the group traveled three thousand miles, meeting average Chinese workers, visiting homes, nurseries, and hospitals, and filming as much as they could.

MacLaine was impressed with what she saw, most particularly with the sense of calm and purpose that she found in the Chinese people. "The Chinese believe they can do anything. That's the whole secret of that revolution."[30] She attributes this to the emphasis on cooperation, which has become government policy over the years. For MacLaine it's like having "800,000,000 in group therapy." Having witnessed the destructive elements in Western society, the Chinese experience gave her a chance to reevaluate her own values. MacLaine states emphatically that she is not a Maoist but feels that China is the only country in the world that is radical in its social structure. She believes that they offer an alternative to the competitive society that is strangling *our* culture. However, she is the first to admit that she could not live in such a puritanic society that lacks controversy and free artistic expression.

All of these sentiments come through most clearly in her own account of the Chinese trip, covered in *You Can Get There From Here*. The book also relates her experiences on the campaign trail, the filming of *Shirley's World,* and the making of *The Other Half of the Sky: A China Memoir.* It ends with Shirley walking into a dance studio for the first time in twenty years.

MacLaine's return to dancing marked another 360-degree turn: a commitment to do what she did best. While she spent hours at her desk writing *You Can Get There From Here,* the first draft of which ran five-thousand pages, she also prepared herself physically to return to the stage where she had started. After months of dieting, jogging, and much practice, she opened in Las Vegas in a show called "If They Could See Me Now." The show was a colossal success and prompted MacLaine to do several television programs.

"The Gypsy in My Soul," aired on 20 January 1976, was dedicated to all hoofers and chorus liners—called "gypsies." The show ended with a free-for-all in which members of the television audience (anyone with a union equity card) were invited to come onto the floor and perform.

Following the television special, MacLaine took the five dancers and went on tour. Together they visited twelve European cities, including London, Paris, and Hamburg, and Mexico City. Reviews were not merely glowing but almost hysterical. In London, MacLaine broke the house record at The Palladium, surpassing Danny Kaye, a British favorite. When the show played New York, she made box-office news at The Palace. Much of the audience enthusiasm was based on a response to MacLaine's informal chatter, as well as to the songs that contained personal references.

After the show closed, MacLaine began work on a new film in August, 1976, her first movie in five years. Co-starring Anne Bancroft and premier danseur Mikhail Baryshnikov, the plot centers on two former dancers and a young ballerina coping with love and her career. Directed by ex-choreographer Herbert Ross, the film went into release in 1977.

Other projects still await conclusion. MacLaine is writing a third book—this time a novel. Although she is fairly closemouthed about the contents, she admits it is a very sexy book about a woman who does all the things she wished she had done. She claims that if it's filmed, she would like to play the lead.

Another project close to her heart is a film biography of Amelia Earhart, based on a script by Pete Hamill. The picture was one that both had wanted to make for a long time. MacLaine, who admires Earhart tremendously, had thought of playing the role as early as 1966, but felt she was too young. Now forty-two, she is perfect for the role of the aviatrix.

> She was a woman who early on found out what she wanted to do with her life and did it. Men were important to her but didn't submerge her identity. I've been learning to fly for the role and have researched the movie in the FBI files and in Tokyo. I'm convinced that she was not just on a stunt trip when she died. She and her navigator Fred Noonan, were the first casualties of World War II. She was on a secret mission for Roosevelt.[31]

Hamill wrote the screenplay in 1975. However, difficulty in raising the necessary backing and the television film starring Susan Clark caused delays. Hamill feels that the made-for-TV film was a total ripoff, rushed into production after the announcement and publicity of their project. The two are still hoping to get the film off the ground and then to shoot in the Far East. Hopefully, seventy percent of the footage would be shot on location in the Pacific.

Beyond these projects, the future is unpredictable. Whatever MacLaine does it will be stamped with her own unique personality and filled with contradictions. As she has stated, "I can get up on that stage with long legs and zircon dresses and still be a feminist."[32]

She is outspoken about the dearth of good roles for women: "Strong women have intimidated the creative fantasies in Hollywood. Men are afraid to expose their own chauvinism so they write about males." Yet, MacLaine doesn't consider herself a liberated woman. She told David Hartman on "Good Morning America", "I don't know any liberated woman, any liberated man, any liberated child. No. I guess children are more liberated than any of us and then we grind the little buggers down."[33] She also is the first to admit that she is still very attached to things.

As for politics, MacLaine claims she has her interests on "hold." Commenting on the 1976 candidates, she stated that it was hard to get involved when no one stood for anything.

But whatever MacLaine does, one thing remains consistent: she never loses her sense of humor. Referring to the vast number of scripts people send her every week, she said, "Oh yes, and I got a script about a woman who has an affair with her son. He kills her and eats her. I thought that could make a musical comedy."[34]

2

The Trouble with Harry

Filming began in Vermont in early autumn 1954 to take full advantage of the glorious colors of a New England fall. MacLaine, only days removed from the New York chorus line, headed north with a new husband in tow to meet the inimical Alfred Hitchcock.

Feeling out of her element, MacLaine was totally unfamiliar with movieland lingo and had not yet become accustomed to thinking of herself as a star. Nonchalantly she lunched under the trees with the crew members — her only friends. Hitchcock took her by the hand and led her to the table reserved for the notables, with the advice, "You are a star. If you want it, you must act it."[1] MacLaine listened, but, as in other things, she followed her own course of action, setting a new pattern for stars who would not act the part. Unconcerned about the proprieties and traditions of stardom, MacLaine maintained her down-to-earth affability and managed to gain twenty-five pounds by the end of shooting.

The Trouble With Harry was an unusual picture, even within the Hitchcock repertory. Compared with the complicated crime stories, *The Trouble With Harry* possessed a minimal plot. In contrast to the spine-chilling suspense thrillers, *The Trouble With Harry* is a low-keyed, slow-paced, mellow comedy about death. Hitchcock told the French critic François Truffaut, "*The Trouble With Harry* is an approach to a strictly British genre, the humor of the macabre. I made that picture to prove that the American public could appreciate British humor."[2]

The story begins as four-year-old Arnie Rogers (Jerry Mathers) wanders aimlessly through the forest with his space gun. Suddenly three shots ring out and Arnie stumbles upon the huge body of a dead man. When he returns with his mother Jennifer (MacLaine), she recognizes the corpse as her estranged second husband, Harry. Casually unconcerned, the two leave the dead man on the path.

After Jennifer has departed, old Captain Albert Wiles (Edmund Gwenn) finds Harry's body. Believing he has accidently killed Harry while shooting rabbits (before the hunting season, no less), he contemplates how to dispose of the evidence.

While the Captain hides behind a tree, a passing tramp steals Harry's shoes, and the absentminded, nearsighted Dr. Greenbow trips over the body without even seeing it.

Captain Wiles is in the midst of pulling Harry out of the woods when old Mildred Gravely (Mildred Natwick) appears. When she calmly inquires, "What seems to be the trouble?", Wiles explains his predicament, and Miss Gravely agrees to help him — after a cup of warm tea and some blueberry muffins, however.

Before the two have a chance to bury the body,

43

The Trouble with Harry—with Edmund Gwenn.

The Trouble with Harry—with John Forsythe.

Sam Marlow (John Forsythe), an unsuccessful, local painter, chances upon Harry and sets about reproducing him in oils. The Captain finds Sam in the midst of his work, confesses his crime, thus playing upon Sam's sympathy. The two bury Harry among the maple trees.

Meanwhile, a tramp has caused suspicion with his new shoes, and the local deputy sheriff is on the trail of a corpse he seems unable to locate. Miss Gravely confesses to the Captain that actually she killed Harry when she hit him on the head with her hiking boot. The two decide it would be best to exhume him.

When they tell Sam of their deed, he convinces them that Harry's corpse may provoke a public scandal for both Miss Gravely and Jennifer, and so the three rebury the body. However, Jennifer and Sam, now in love, want to marry and need a corpse to prove her widowhood. So the group digs up Harry for the second time.

By this point, Harry has become rather frayed, and the group decides to take him to Jennifer's house for refurbishing. While they are tidying Harry, Dr. Greenbow passes through and diagnoses the cause of death as a heart attack.

Meanwhile, Sam receives an offer from a visiting millionaire for all of his paintings, providing sufficient funds for he and Jennifer to wed.

The Trouble with Harry—with John Forsythe.

Simultaneously, the Captain proposes to Miss Gravely.

Relieved of guilt, united in new relationships, the group returns Harry to the woods so that Arnie can once again discover the body.

This offbeat farce opened in New York in November 1955. MacLaine has referred to the film as "an artistic bomb, highly subtle in its humor, but nonetheless a bomb."[3] American critics were baffled by what Philip T. Hartung of *Commonweal* called "the thinnest picture Hitchcock has made."[4] Audiences found the leisurely pace too slow for their liking, and even the beauties of Vermont in full color VistaVision proved insufficient to draw crowds.

Reviews in London were more favorable. Critics were tickled by Hitchcock's autumnal gallows humor. *The Spectator* said, "John Michael Hayes's script was written with the bland civilized lunacy of a latter-day Mad Hatter."[5] *The New Statesman* claimed, "The whole film is enchanting, and for

the first time in his career — in his own mellow fall — Hitchcock reveals a touch of poetry."[6] And British critic Penelope Houston wrote, "Harry exists merely as an inapposite feature in an idyllic pastoral scene. Quietly concentrated, the film's humor is largely a matter of a balance precariously sustained; the blazing splendour of the landscape set off the grim little joke of a plot."[7] In Paris, this unpretentious little film did even better. Finding popular support, it ran for six months at a small theater on the Champs-Elysées.

As MacLaine's debut work, the film had mixed results. She drew good reviews, a fact to be repeated time and time again in the future despite the bad press of many of the movies. *Films in Review* stated that Hitchcock "makes effective use of a new actress whose face, mannerisms and speech are a compound of the fey, the young, and the sometimes beautiful."[8] Certainly *The Trouble With Harry* marked MacLaine as someone to be watched, although it did not skyrocket her to immediate success. Hal Wallis, with whom Mac-Laine was under contract, unsure as to how to best utilize her talents, kept her on tap.

But *The Trouble With Harry* did go a long way in establishing one side of the MacLaine persona — the forthright, ingenuous lass who seemed a natural as the girl next door. Hitchcock managed to tap this aspect of MacLaine—the warm smile, the quizzical glance—and to transfer it successfully onto the screen. Later films would develop other sides of her personality.

3

Artists and Models

Artists and Models, MacLaine's second film, released one month after *The Trouble With Harry,* was her first experience in a Hal Wallis Production. With little liking for the role and even less for Wallis's treatment, which deemed all artists as merchandise, she went into the project with less than heartfelt enthusiasm.

Artists and Models was also MacLaine's first film with Dean Martin. Together they were to appear in five films and to become life-long friends. This relationship and MacLaine's initiation into the so-called Rat Pack did not really blossom, however, until the filming of *Some Came Running,* starring Frank Sinatra and Dean Martin. There, isolated from the rest of the world in the quiet town of Madison, Indiana, the actors had many long hours to get to know one another. Proving she could hold her own at gin rummy, MacLaine quickly became a favorite and the only female member allowed in The Clan.

Artists and Models is a typical Dean Martin-Jerry Lewis vehicle, with some wonderful touches and in-jokes by director and co-author Frank Tashlin. The basic outline concerns the efforts of Martin and Lewis, referred to as "two Greenwich Village nitwits" by Bosley Crowther in *The New York Times,* to find love and fortune in the competitive world of pulp publishing.

As Rick Todd, Martin plays nursemaid to Eugene Fullstack (Lewis) while trying to succeed as a serious artist. Eugene aspires to be a children's author but has disturbing nightmares induced by the reams of comic books he consumes daily. During the day, he fantasizes about the love of his life — Bat Lady.

Having lost their last job (billboard painting), the two apply for work at Murdock Books, publishers of the famed Bat Lady Comics. While there, Rick meets Abigail Parker (Dorothy Malone), creator of Bat Lady, and begins a passionate pursuit that eventually proves successful. Eugene meets Mr. Murdock's bouncy secretary, Bessie Sparrowbush (MacLaine), who goes after him with a vengeance. Eugene doesn't recognize Bessie as the model for his ideal heroine.

Rick lands a job by submitting gory material he has lifted from Eugene, who talks in his sleep. Success seems assured until the United States Army detects their own top-secret plans in Murdock's new comic book *Vincent the Vulture.* The Russians also pick up the trail and send their spy, Sonia (Eva Gabor), to get the rest of the formula.

The film culminates at the Artists and Models Ball. Following a big production number, Sonia helps kidnap Bessie and takes her costume. Dressed as Bat Lady she easily entices Eugene (who is wearing his Freddie the Fieldmouse costume) to an

Artists and Models—with Jerry Lewis.

abandoned mansion, where thugs are waiting to pry the secrets from Eugene. Rick finds Bessie, and together they rush to save Eugene. Returning to the ball in time for the big finale, the four leads happily pair off as the camera slowly tracks away.

Despite the jaundiced look at the world of cartoon creation (a world quite familiar to Tashlin who had worked in animation offscreen and on since 1930), the plot serves as little more than a clothesline on which to hang songs for Dean Martin and comic situations for Jerry Lewis. Some of the material holds up rather well, even after twenty years. Two scenes in particular stand out—both with strong overtones of Marx Brothers' comedy. One is a silent pantomime (reminiscent of Harpo, for whom Tashlin had once worked) by Lewis, who tries to communicate with Martin, using hand gestures. The other is a session on a massage table, which grows into a tangle involving five twisted bodies. The confusion recalls the zany stateroom sequence in *A Night at the Opera*. There is also a nice number entitled "When You Pretend," which is filled with clever filmic gags typical of Tashlin ingenuity.

As Bessie, MacLaine plays upon the same pixie image she innovated in *The Trouble With Harry*.

Sporting short red hair, she bats her eyes and smiles incessantly. However, for *Artists and Models* a new element was added: sex. Disregarding her prim little blouse and childlike voice, Bessie seems to have little upstairs except a desire to get her hands on Eugene. To this end she literally attacks him, pinning him to the wall with a kiss that makes the top of his shoes pop up. What she sees in the juvenile Eugene is hard to fathom, for despite her own shallowness, she is light-years beyond him.

MacLaine cared little for the role of Bessie and expressed a certain resentment about the use of women as sex objects. In an interview, she told reporter Albert Johnson, "all I had to do was to walk up and down some stairs." *In Don't Fall Off the Mountain*, she writes:

> Just as I had always suspected, the yellow sunsuit was for me. I was the one who ran in and out of scenes yelling, "Which way did they go?" And, when I finally did find Jerry (I got Jerry; the other actress got Dean), I was supposed to jump on him and hold him down. I represented all the plain broads in the audience who could never get a man unless they pinned him to the floor. I guess that's when I first realized it was possible to make people laugh and cry at the same time.[1]

From the opening credits (replete with live models who look like statues) to the closing gala, the film is filled with glamorous dames who do little more than strut about showing off their best features in hopes of pleasing a man. Abigail, the only female with an ounce of intelligence, is made to appear sexually repressed because she values her career and doesn't immediately succumb to Martin's romantic overtures. Her later submission is predictable, however, in this male romance. As a comic antidote to Abigail, Bessie is portrayed as the sexual aggressor, but no more realistically; she goes after Eugene with the sensitivity of a Mack truck.

The film was MacLaine's first chance to sing on the screen. Dressed in the aforementioned yellow sunsuit, she takes up the refrain of Martin's *Innamorata*. Although her voice is thin, she puts the song across with joyful abandon, as she simultaneously drapes herself on the staircase, hangs from the bannister, and stretches her long legs—all in an effort to attract Eugene's attention. The voice might easily have been dubbed, but the distinctive MacLaine inflections were clearly preferable.

Artists and Models

Artists and Models—Dean Martin, Jerry Lewis, Shirley MacLaine, and Dorothy Malone.

Artists and Models was the fourteenth film Martin and Lewis made together. Two films and two years later each went off in his own direction.

As for MacLaine, she went off with Michael Todd to film *Around the World in Eighty Days*.

4

Around the World in 80 Days

Having starred in one commercial disaster and playing a supporting role in another success, MacLaine's third film, Mike Todd's extravaganza *Around the World in 80 Days*, was to make movie history. As one of the world's great showmen, Todd had dreams of grandeur, matched only by his boundless energy and personal magnetism. MacLaine has described him as "a five-foot-five concentration of human spark."[1] Todd came on the Hollywood scene during the death throes of the studio system and the battle of the big screen, and he threw his talents into creating what he hoped would be the greatest picture ever made—certainly one of the biggest and most expensive.

To achieve this goal, he budgeted an unheard of $7,000,000 (some sources claim more) to shoot a film in the newly devised widescreen process named Todd-AO. Todd-AO, which projected a 70mm print onto a 26' by 60' curved screen, accompanied by six-channel sound, had two advantages over Cinerama (first publicly unveiled in 1952): first, it utilized only one projector (instead of three); and second, it produced a sharper, clearer image. Shooting for the grand spectacular was planned for twenty-five locations around the world, in addition to the five or six studio backlots. As a consummate businessman, however, Todd didn't believe in wasting money when he didn't have to; therefore, he made use of ready-made studio sets whenever possible.

Todd had noted the limitations of pure spectacles like Cinerama (in which he had been a backer), and he was determined to find a first-rate property that would engage his audiences and hold their attention. For this Todd chose Jules Verne's classic adventure novel *Around the World in 80 Days*. The story had the merits of combining good suspense with multifarious characters and settings. On film it became a virtual travelogue that featured exotic places, breathtaking vistas, and a constant change of scenery.

For his leads Todd chose David Niven as the intrepid Phileas Fogg, the epitome of the proper Englishman, and the Mexican actor, Cantinflas, as his comic valet, Passepartout. Combining all of the necessary elements for an extravaganza *par excellence*, he then signed over forty-five notable stars for minor roles. Most of these actors, like Marlene Dietrich, Frank Sinatra, Charles Boyer, Ronald Coleman, Hermione Gingold, and Beatrice Lillie, agreed to make guest appearances as a special favor to Todd. Lastly, with typical Todd unpredictability and *chutzpa*, he selected MacLaine, a virtual newcomer, for the entrusted role of leading lady.

The choice of MacLaine for a Hindu princess was certainly a strange one. One commentator referred to it as a "spectacular piece of miscasting." But MacLaine was tickled with the role.

Around the World in Eighty Days—with David Niven.

When she asked Todd why he had chosen a freckled-faced redhead, he replied that he wanted a campy Hindu princess. Later he commented, "She's believable, yet has that pixie quality."[2]

The plot of *Around the World in 80 Days* concerns the efforts of Phileas Fogg, a nineteenth-century gentleman, to make good a wager that he can circle the globe in eighty days. Leaving London, he travels eastward with his clever valet, Passepartout, picking up others temporarily along the way. Inspector Fix (Robert Newton) becomes a permanent follower, who deceptively believes he is following an important bank robber.

In India the two light upon Princess Aouda. Fogg first spies the princess through the bushes as she is being carried to her death. As is the custom, she is expected to commit *sutee* (suicide on the funeral pyre of her late husband). Young and beautiful, she is at first sadly resigned to her fate; but as the moment of death draws near, she struggles to be free. Fogg and Passepartout determine to rescue her. Disguised as the Rajah, Passepartout appears, frightening off the natives, who believe the Rajah has returned to life.

The group, with the addition of Aouda, now proceeds to Hong Kong. On board the S.S. Rangoon, Aouda listens attentively as Fogg explains the rules of whist, and then, in perfect English (she was educated in Britain), she tells him of her past life. Quietly Aouda tries to change Fogg's stuffy formality.

The three move on to Yokohama and then to San Francisco's Barbary Coast. There Fogg shields Aouda's eyes to prevent her from observing the obscene saloon girls with their skirts up. But Aouda, fascinated by all native customs, wants to watch. As the group moves eastward aboard an iron horse, Aouda and Fogg pass the time at whist. After sustaining an Indian attack and other misadventures, the group finally boards a liner at New York harbor, back for England.

In London, Fogg dejectedly discovers that he

The lovely princess in *Around the World in Eighty Days.*

has missed the deadline. Ever the optimist, Aouda tries to cheer him up. First she blames herself for their delay in India. Then, announcing that misfortune is always easier if shared, she proposes marriage. Jubilantly, Fogg accepts, adding an apology for his present penury.

As the two make wedding preparations, Fogg realizes that he has miscalculated the date and rushes off to the Reform Club to make a grand entrance. Aouda follows close behind. The appearance of a woman at this all-male club horrifies the members. When Aouda bewilderedly questions why women are excluded from this male domain, she is told, "Because that could spell the end of the British Empire." Making a special exception, the members relent and all ends happily.

Around the World in 80 Days opened at the Rivoli Theatre in New York on 18 October 1956. Reviewers, who seldom have kind words for the "big pictures," all praised the film. *Films in Review* was most ecstatic.

> I think it niggling of the New York critics to call *Around the World in 80 Days* merely a blockbuster of a show. P.T. Barnum's old line "the greatest show on earth" is not too much to call this landmark of motion picture history.[3]

Responses from audiences were equally enthusiastic. The first year, the film grossed a whopping $16,200,000, spiraling it up to the top of the all-time box-office champs, right under *Gone With the Wind*. In 1959 it moved down to fourth place, behind *The Ten Commandments* and *The Robe*, where it remained until 1966.

At the 1957 Academy Awards presentations, *Around the World* walked off with five Oscars: cinematography, editing, music, writing, and Best Picture of the Year. Over the years the film has brought in $23,000,000, fulfilling Todd's dream of creating one of the biggest blockbusters of all time. Unhappily, his death in an airplane crash in 1958 put an end to his amazing career.

The character of Princess Aouda had much in common with MacLaine's own personality. She was intelligent and curious, casual and outspoken, and antiestablishment to the core. Aouda was not afraid to initiate a marriage proposal, and her whist playing seems like a foreshadowing of MacLaine's own addiction to gin rummy.

The scene at the Reform Club plays like an episode from MacLaine's autobiography. However, embedded in the comic episode there exists a serious subject that was only beginning to surface in the midfifties. This scene not only exposes the absurdity of an all-male institution, but it also demonstrates through the members' own responses the degree to which any change threatens the whole social structure of a male society.

Although most of the critics praised the acting of the principles, performances were hardly the primary interest in a film that offered so many distractions for the eye and ear. Few critics commented specifically on MacLaine, except to concur that she had been miscast. Black hair and makeup did little to cover her fresh American features or mask her ingénue voice. But MacLaine was not pleased with her awkward performance and recognized that, though she might have natural talents as a comedienne, acting might take a lot more practice.

Despite the success of *Around the World* and MacLaine's wide exposure, the film did little to advance her career. In fact, her career actually took a downslide, sending her back to singing and dancing on several television shows. For acting experience she took a role in a road company of *The Sleeping Prince*.

Meanwhile, MacLaine gave birth to a baby girl, Stephanie Sachiko Parker. Born 1 September 1956, the child was named after a Japanese orphan that Parker had cared for after the war.

For the next two years, MacLaine worked sporatically, cared for Sachie, and waited patiently for the producers to telephone.

5

Hot Spell

In *Hot Spell*, released May 1958, MacLaine was cast in a supporting role as Shirley Booth's daughter. In one respect, this was a step downward after two starring roles; on the other hand, it offered her a fine opportunity to tackle a serious, dramatic role after the nonsensical frolics in *Artists and Models* and *Around the World in 80 Days*.

The movie had two things that appealed to MacLaine. One was a chance to work with Daniel Mann, the director who had filmed her screen test and who had directed Shirley Booth in her Academy Award winning performance, *Come Back, Little Sheba* (1952). Second was a chance to test her acting ability on the screen. Although *The Sleeping Prince* was rather short-lived, the reviews were decent, and the experience proved she had potential as a dramatic actress.

Set in New Orleans, *Hot Spell* deals with the intricacies of family life in the South. In theme it differs little from the body of terse, little melodramas about sex and frustration that filled the screen during the fifties. A goodly number were set in small towns (especially in the South) and, like *Hot Spell*, were based on stage dramas. The list, beginning with *Come Back, Little Sheba*, includes *Picnic* (1955), *The Rose Tatoo* (1955), *Baby Doll* (1956), *Bus Stop* (1956), *Wild is the Wind* (1957), *Cat on a Hot Tin Roof* (1958), *Home Before Dark* (1958), and *The Long, Hot Summer* (1958).

One-half of these works concentrate on the figure of an aging heroine.

The plot of *Hot Spell* concerns the members of the Duval family. Jack Duval (Anthony Quinn), a rough-mannered forty-five-year-old realtor, has long since lost interest in his dumpy, nonassertive wife and has taken up with a younger woman. Despite her loneliness, Alma Duval (Shirley Booth) deludes herself into thinking that everything is fine. She spends most of the day pampering her family, which no longer needs her. The two sons, Buddy (Earl Holliman) and Billy (Clint Kimbrough), each have become estranged from the family. Buddy wants to make a real-estate killing to prove he is his father's equal but is rebuked by his father's demeaning comments. Billy has turned to books in a complete rejection of Jack's values. Only Virginia (MacLaine) seems to hold any real affection for her parents. Although she, like her brothers, knows of Jack's affairs and sees the futility of her mother's deceptions, Ginny is the only one who sympathizes with her mother's situation.

The film is structured around various family confrontations: Alma's request to return to New Paris (the place where she and Jack spent the first happy years of their marriage); Buddy's quarrel with his father; Jack's outburst at Virginia and later his anger at Billy. Eventually, Jack gets fed up

Hot Spell—with Shirley Booth.

and leaves town with his girlfriend Ruby.

For once the family is united, as they wait for the telephone call from Jack. The call comes, but only to inform them that Jack and Ruby have been killed in a highway accident. After so many years, Alma finally returns to New Paris. But things are no longer as they were. Only after Jack's funeral does she realize that one can never really go back. Less sentimental than before, she boards the train with her family to return to New Orleans.

As Virginia, MacLaine plays one of her few roles as a screen daughter (in almost every other film she appears *sans familia*). *The Sheepman* and *Career* both contain father figures and no mothers, but the role of daughter is highly minimized. In *The Sheepman*, MacLaine functions completely independently, and, in *Career*, she and the father never even appear in a single scene together. In *Hot Spell* she is integrated into the family circle: part child, part adult — perched on the brink of womanhood.

In the role of Virginia, MacLaine demonstrates her greatest assets—a vibrant alacrity and a natural sweetness. The acting of the entire cast was beyond reproach, and MacLaine turned in her best performance to date. Young and alive, she managed to be engaging without becoming clawingly cute.

Having rejected her steadfast boyfriend, Harry, for a more exciting, sophisticated medical student, Ginny seeks an intimacy that she never shared with Harry. Afraid of being too receptive but anxious to please, Ginny responds shyly, then more passionately, to Wyatt's advances. Like her mother, she is humiliated by Jack's questions about Wyatt's intentions. Embarrassed, she escapes to her room in tears. It is only later in the woods that Ginny discovers Wyatt's real motives. Wyatt praises Ginny's honesty, then ignoring her, confesses his intention to marry someone with money and position. Again, reduced to tears, she flees home.

The film's misogynist attitudes operate on two

levels—within and outside of the film. Jack and Wyatt both reveal male-chauvinist tendencies and seem unable to relate to women as other than sources of pleasure or objects of use.

Beyond the context of the plot, the film *does* raise the important question of momism. Alma has dedicated her life to the role of wife and mother and finds little reward for her devotion. Implicit in the characterization is a rejection of domestic values. Further, there is also an implication that (taken to its extreme) such values are destructive. It is easy to conclude that Jack's death is a direct result of Alma's inability to satisfy his male needs.

The problem is worthy of serious consideration. Unfortunately, the film never fully deals with the broader social aspects, such as causes, education, or alternatives. However, Alma's condition, never fully analyzed, is used as an excuse to make Jack's behavior believable. Despite Booth's long scene alone, she is never able to make Alma into more than a lonely, pathetic character.

Only as a countermodel for Ginny does Alma serve any constructive function. Ginny's brief fling has proved that tarts and tramps are not the only women treated as objects. Clearly, men like Wyatt find it quite convenient to further their careers at the expense of emotional bonds. If the episode has proved painful, it has taught Ginny something of the facts of life. Unwilling to compromise herself, Ginny rejects a love affair with Wyatt. Ginny returns to Harry, choosing security over adventure. Wiser to the ways of the world, she will not make the same mistakes as her mother.

6

The Sheepman

After *Hot Spell*, MacLaine made two films before achieving stardom in *Some Came Running*. The films were *The Sheepman* (1958) and *The Matchmaker* (1958). From MacLaine's point of view, these projects simply served to mark time. She states in her autobiography, "I finished *Hot Spell* and went on from one insignificant picture to another."[1] Actually, *The Sheepman* is a perfectly enjoyable, well-crafted, comic Western made by the veteran Hollywood director George Marshall. Modest in every aspect, it attempts little more than to provide an entertaining story that good-naturedly pokes fun at some of the Western clichés. Together, *Destry Rides Again* (1939), *Red Garters* (1954), and *The Sheepman* (also released as *Stranger With a Gun*) constitute a small body of work done by Marshall that attempts to elaborate the comic possibilities of the genre. These films appeared before the self-conscious era of the late sixties, and they are precursors to the broader parodies like *Cat Ballou* (1965), *Support Your Local Sheriff* (1969), and the spaghetti Westerns of Sergio Leone.

In terms of her career, the character of Dell Patton in *The Sheepman* offered MacLaine the opportunity to play an intelligent, independent woman, as well as to develop the MacLaine persona, typified by an offhand, nonchalant manner. Critical response to MacLaine's performance was consistently laudatory. In fact, *Films in Review* felt that her portrayal was a step forward after *The Trouble With Harry* and *Hot Spell*.

The plot concerns the efforts of easygoing Jason Sweet (Glenn Ford) to bring sheep into the cattle lands of Powder Valley. Arriving by train during the 1880s, Jason quickly establishes himself as a man with punch behind his words. Dell, a headstrong young lady, warns him that the citizens are content with the status quo, so Jason seeks out Colonel Stephen Bedford, the town's leading citizen and Dell's fiancé.

It develops that Jason and Bedford (Leslie Nielsen), former ally Johnny Bledsoe, are old friends with a personal score to settle, and that each has a past he prefers to hide. Despite Bedford's threats, Jason unloads his sheep at the local depot, aided by some frightened Mexicans and the timely explosion of several sticks of firecrackers. For awhile all is peaceful. Jason is even invited to the local Fourth of July dance. The invitation however, proves to be just a ruse to railroad him and his assistant, Milt, out-of-town — a plot that Dell helps to engineer.

Jason returns to town and exposes Bedford's underhanded business dealings, thus winning local support. After killing Bedford's three henchmen, with assistance from Dell and Milt, Jason heads for the mansion for a final showdown with his old

The Sheepman—with Glenn Ford.

The Sheepman—with Glenn Ford and Edgar Buchanan.

buddy. Bedford is killed, and the film ends with a repartee between Jason and Dell. Having decided to stay in Powder Valley, Jason has exchanged his sheep for cattle and plans to settle down with Dell.

Unlike Marlene Dietrich in *Destry Rides Again*, the character of Dell Patton possesses both backbone and beauty without the necessary sacrifice of her good name. Neither barroom tramp nor God-fearing wife — the two stock female types in most Westerns — Dell is a perfect blend of feminine and masculine traits. She is able to hold her own in a man's world without losing her femininity, characterizing the true strength of the pioneer women. Even her physical acts (shooting a hired gunman) are performed in a graceful manner. In this regard she is a softer, low-keyed version of Barbara Stanwyck's high-powered heroine in *Forty Guns*, made the previous year.

Dell's decision to warn Jason of potential danger shows both an independent mind and a compassionate heart. She refers to this warning as her "own stupid idea," a self-deprecative remark that has little relevance in this film, but which becomes a hallmark of MacLaine's later portrayals (especially in *The Apartment, Two For the Seesaw*, and *Sweet Charity*). Although Dell freely expresses her own opinions, her willing acceptance of the dominant ideology of the cattle society demonstrates her inability to look beyond the limitations of the patriarchal system. Without stretching the point too far, the demands of the sheepmen for an open grazing range is not unlike the threat posed to society by feminist challenges for more representation. The masculine qualities of the cattle versus the passive qualities of the sheep follows this same line of reasoning.

Symbolic of Dell's worth is the respect with which the male characters treat her. In terms of the film, this makes her a fitting partner for Jason, a man of character and determination. Like Jason, however, Dell is not above using deception when it is to her advantage. Happily, nowhere in the film is this equated with destructive, feminine wiles; rather, it serves to forge a bond between the two protagonists. As Jason tells Dell, "I'm like you. When I'm the nicest is when you have to watch the closest."

Despite MacLaine's whiney voice, which often sounds both juvenile and grating, her sassy dialogue and quick responses establish her as a self-assured woman of the West. Her naturalness and honesty seem in perfect keeping with the freedom of the new land. Her long red hair, which contrasted her masculine clothing, projected a feminine look MacLaine had not previously shown on the screen.

Although both MacLaine and Ford play their roles with a sense of ironic aloofness (MacLaine's quizzical looks punctuate the action like a double take), the main comedy falls to the minor characters — especially Mickey Shaughnessy in the role of the brute, Jumbo McCall. *The New York Times* did point out, though, that MacLaine's "blissful nonchalance in times of crisis and her casualness with frivolous remarks help to preserve the tone of mockery that is the nicest thing about this film."[2]

After the swipes at the established male order, it is regrettable that the ending of the film is so reactionary. Having opened the land for sheep, Jason instead chooses to raise cattle. For her part, Dell, having lived a life of self-determination, agrees to allow Jason to rule the house, although the pretense of such an arrangement is clearly revealed. Despite the intended irony, perhaps no interchange during the fifties reveals more clearly the absurdity of traditional role-playing than the ending of the *Sheepman.* Jason has just advised Dell of his intention to make all of the decisions for their household. He symbolically takes the carriage reigns from Dell and, in response to her suggestion to back up, says, "I'll decide what to do." In comic fashion, he decides to back up. The point is well made, and no one remains fooled as to where the real authority resides; one simply questions the necessity of the sham and wonders about the ultimate price to the female ego.

7

The Matchmaker

The Matchmaker (1958) was MacLaine's second film with Shirley Booth and her first effort with director Joseph Anthony, who directed her again in *Career* and *All in a Night's Work*. Although Anthony never distinguished himself as an individualist of note, he did elicit good performances from his actors.

The decision to film the 1938 Thorton Wilder comedy is certainly questionable; however, Anthony dealt competently with the period play. Reviewers seemed divided concerning the suitability of adapting farce for the screen and differed widely in their reactions to the theatrical asides spoken directly to the film audience. However, for the summer of 1958, most approached the movie as a pleasant diversion that could be enjoyed for its old-fashioned charms. Filmed in black and white, it lacks the pazazz of the later musical version, *Hello Dolly* (1969), starring Barbra Streisand.

Set in Yonkers, 1884, the story centers on the exploits of Dolly Levi (Shirley Booth), a matchmaker who sets her sights on Horace Vandergelder (Paul Ford), Yonker's wealthiest and thriftiest old fool. Disguising her intentions, Dolly presumes to make a match for Vandergelder with a charming, young milliner, Irene Molloy (MacLaine), who lives in New York City.

Vandergelder takes off for the City, leaving his two clerks Cornelius Hackl (Anthony Perkins) and Barnaby Tucker (Robert Morse) in charge of the store. Experiencing their first taste of freedom, the two young men decide to visit the City themselves in hopes of an exciting adventure. Accidentally they arrive at Miss Molloy's hat shop. Cornelius poses as a wealthy Yonker's rake until he is forced to hide when Vandergelder and Dolly appear. Vandergelder eventually discovers the two surreptitious visitors and storms out.

Believing the stories Cornelius has told her, Irene insists on a fancy dinner at the Harmonia Club as compensation for her compromised position. Inviting her friend Minnie for Barnaby, the four set out for an evening on the town. Meanwhile, Dolly has interested Vandergelder in a new prospect, Ernestina Simple, and they also go to the Harmonia Club to wait for the fictitious Ernestina to arrive. By a complex turn of events, Cornelius acquires Vandergelder's lost wallet, enabling him to pay for the expensive meal before high-tailing it back to Yonkers. When Vandergelder discovers the double deception, he leaves Dolly and returns to Yonkers.

Undaunted, Dolly helps Cornelius establish his own rival business, which quickly brings Vandergelder to his knees. In a sudden change of heart, Vandergelder agrees to rehire Cornelius at a substantial increase in salary and humbly proposes to Dolly. Cornelius gets Irene, Barnaby gets Minnie, and all ends happily as it should. The film closes

The Matchmaker—with Anthony Perkins and Robert Morse.

The Matchmaker—with Anthony Perkins.

The Matchmaker—with Anthony Perkins.

with each character offering his own moral, while Dolly assures the viewers that a good adventure is worth a little risk.

The film is filled with the witty aphorisms and cogent advise that marked the Thurber original. Well aware of the sexual politics in human relations, Vandergelder notes: "Marriage is a bribe to make a housekeeper think she's a house-holder." As a working woman, Dolly has other ideas. Concerning money she states that "Money is like manure; it should be spread around."

MacLaine also plays a working woman. Though less aggressive than Dolly, she too acknowledges the problems of getting by without a man. In particular she resents the common currency that labels all milliners as wicked and passionate women.

MacLaine was well-suited for the role of Irene Molloy. Looking thinner than in her previous films, she captures the delicate charm of the Victorian era without losing her own natural spontaneity. *Variety* called her "pert and lovely"; *The New York Times*, "sweet, demure and confused." Even her raucous laugh is toned down to a refined giggle. MacLaine's positive optimism infects the Molloy character and enervates her decision to "make the most" of a ruined reputation. Staying within the confines of gentle humor, she uses her face to full advantage. When Cornelius puts his arm around her waist, the expression that registers across her countenance is like a slowly dawning sun. *Films in Review* predicted, "If in the next few years she (MacLaine) learns as much as she has in the last two or three, she should be one of the most popular actresses of the next decade."[1]

8

Some Came Running

Some Came Running, directed by Vincente Minnelli, was shot on location in Madison, Indiana, and was released in February, 1959. As Ginny Moorhead, MacLaine fulfilled the promise Hal Wallis and Alfred Hitchcock had seen in her four years back. Ginny became the prototype for all the subsequent hookers MacLaine portrayed on the American screen.

The story, based on a sprawling melodramatic novel by James Jones (author of *From Here to Eternity),* concerns the return of a sensitive ex-serviceman to his home in Parkman, Illinois. Played by Frank Sinatra, Dave Hirsh is a writer of talent but personally rough around the edges. He refuses to conform to the amenities of small-town life and tries to win the intelligent, upper-class Gwen French (Martha Hyer) on his own terms.

In the supporting role of Ginny, MacLaine plays a good-natured but unintelligent tramp whom Dave "picked up" while on a drunken spree. Decked out in a low-cut, short dress, she tumbles off the bus with disheveled red hair, rosy cheeks, and bright red lipstick. Part hussy, part child, she munches on chewing gum, uses the broad "a" typical of Chicago's lower classes, and carries a few belongings in a stuffed animal that serves as a purse.

Ginny takes the opportunity to enjoy herself at the local bar while Dave tries to find a place for himself in the home he left sixteen years ago. She encounters local gambler Bama Diller (Dean

Martin), who superstitiously never removes his hat, and agreeably decides to take up residence at his place, especially since Dave's interests are engaged elsewhere.

Although clearly short on brain power, Ginny has no difficulty sizing up situations correctly. She has genuine feelings for Dave, but realizes these feelings are not reciprocated. Likewise, although her professional experience has taught her the value of being agreeable, and although innately she emanates an innocent sweetness, she reacts demonstratively when she thinks she is being treated unfairly. Shrieking with piercing sounds, she has no inhibitions about expressing her anger.

When Gwen finally rejects Dave's proposal of marriage (recognizing that she is incapable of adjusting to his life-style despite her attraction to his literary talents), Dave returns to Diller and Ginny, hurt and angry.

After a drunken evening on the town, Dave asks Ginny to marry him. She is thrilled by the possibility of setting up house and living with Dave, and promises to be a good wife to him. Dave's motivations are not nearly so simple, however. In part, he is genuinely touched by Ginny's selfless love and admits that no one had ever loved him so before. Feeling sorry for himself, he says that perhaps he can help her since he seems unable to help himself.

On another level, however, Dave's proposal is

Some Came Running

Some Came Running—with Frank Sinatra.

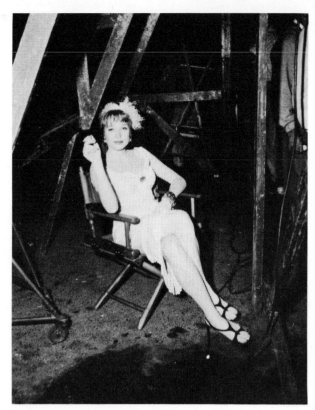

On the set of *Some Came Running.*

extremely sensitive to physical aspects of character. She has stated that "the first thing that I try to do in reading any script is to think of how the person moves. If I know that, everything else falls into place. If I know how she moves her legs, her hands, her head, how she stands—then I can get completely absorbed in the part."[1]

For Ginny this meant wide-eyed looks that indicated her desire to "catch-on," even when a comment was beyond her. It also meant knees that turned in, skirts that hiked up, and hair that was never combed. The combination reflected not just cheap taste appropriate to her background but also an indifference to her appearance, indicating low self-esteem as well as a certain freedom to create her own rules.

It would be easy to discard Ginny as an embarrassment to womanhood, but that would be a shallow response. In fact, in her way, Ginny reflected the unwillingness of even limited individuals to accept the role of unfeeling object. MacLaine has stated that in her view Ginny was a tart, "but nothing if not feminine. She knew how to love. To me that's all important. That was the easiest role I ever played. I only had to read the script once to know the girl inside and out."[2]

MacLaine added dimensions to the character of Ginny that were not apparent in the original novel. In particular she played upon a certain tomboyishness that had always been a part of her own character. Despite MacLaine's comments about Ginny's "femininity," her walk, her manners, and her language all reveal a manner typical of little girls who learn to play with and be accepted by the boys. This freedom from conventional ladylike behavior becomes a trademark of many MacLaine roles.

In accordance with a tomboyish manner, Ginny was not especially sexy. Ginny represented a shoulder to cry on, good times, a swell pal rather than an object of male lust. She listened intently, laughed easily, and always seemed willing to pitch in and help. Perhaps not all was redeemed by "a heart of gold," but as Ginny says, "You don't have to understand to be able to feel." The enormous feeling latent in Ginny's character saved the role from being stereotypical. Her death at the end, a change from the original version, was genuinely moving.

As Minnelli has stated in his book, *I Remember It Well,* Ginny represented the failure of sex rather

simply "love on the rebound." He is seeking relief from the pain inflicted by Gwen and jumps at the first chance to debase himself, hoping this will produce the appropriate guilt feelings in Gwen. Thus, Ginny becomes the tool of Dave's revenge.

The marriage between Dave and Ginny is hardly given time to develop. Following a magnificent carnival sequence, lighted and choreographed in Minnelli's discernable style, Ginny is shot in an effort to shield Dave from the bullet of her jealous, ex-boyfriend. At the funeral Diller pays Ginny a final tribute—he removes his hat.

The film received mixed reviews, though the performances of the leads were well praised. MacLaine was cited for her "wonderful abandon," although some critics felt less engaged by what they termed an "over-written, over-acted" performance. But despite the broad characterizations, typical of later roles as well, *Some Came Running* made MacLaine a star. It particularly emphasized MacLaine's talents for both comedy and drama.

What MacLaine achieved so well was the ability to imply more than she stated. Partly this was achieved through facial expressions and body movements. Having been a dancer, MacLaine is than its triumph. He chose MacLaine for the part because she was not a typical Hollywood bombshell. In directing her, he sought to emphasize the pathetic. Her harsh makeup and flashy clothes were part of a deliberate effort to make her appear obviously vulgar. Exaggeration is what Minnelli wanted and that was what he achieved. As for MacLaine, she received her first Academy Award nomination.

9

Ask Any Girl

Flush from the success of *Some Came Running,* MacLaine filmed *Ask Any Girl,* directed by Charles Walters and released by Metro-Goldwyn-Mayer in May 1959. For the first time in her career MacLaine actually carried a film. Now, no longer a promising personality but a full-fledged star, MacLaine literally dominates the action.

Ask Any Girl was also MacLaine's best opportunity to date to develop fully the comic traits suggested in her early films—the incredulous candor, the joyful abandon, and the whacky unconventionality. *Time* said she possessed the greatest "beauty, talent and mass appeal" since comedienne Carole Lombard.

Ask Any Girl is essentially a male-female entertainment film rooted in the conventions of the screw-ball comedies of the thirties. Based on the battle of the sexes, these works contained fast-paced, sassy dialogue and absurd narrative situations. The women of this genre (played by Carole Lombard, Rosalind Russell, and Katharine Hepburn) were zany and free, easily a match for their male counterparts (usually played by a straight and stuffy Cary Grant). The films were animated by a sense of sexual tension, and because comedy was not considered worthy of "serious" consideration, much passed the Board of Censors, which would have been considered unacceptable in another genre.

During the late fifties these vehicles were resurrected for Doris Day and Rock Hudson, with Day in the male role and Hudson playing the female part. Their first big hit was *Pillow Talk,* made the same year as *Ask Any Girl.* However, compared with the thirties' heroine, both MacLaine and Day seem sexually adolescent—a reflection on the retrogressive ideals of the Eisenhower years. Like the archetypal Day character, MacLaine moves from sexual innocence and puritanical morality (she neither drinks nor smokes) to sexual sophistication—freed from all inhibitions. However, whereas Day always has a glamorous, responsible job that demands initiative and intelligence (interior designer, advertising executive, teacher), MacLaine takes a succession of rather ordinary jobs, which she lands because of her "natural assets"—namely, legs and breasts. Lastly, Day succumbs to marriage (an ambiguous step forward), whereas MacLaine triumphs by getting her man (an ambiguous reward). Initially, then, *Ask Any Girl* hardly seems a challenging vehicle for Hollywood's number-one maverick. However, on closer examination the film reveals some interesting twists that, like the *double entendres* sprinkled neatly throughout the film, work on two levels.

The film opens with a narration by MacLaine in the role of Meg Wheeler. "According to statistics, in the United States there are 5,000,000 more women than men." We are informed that each day 250 of these women arrive in New York searching for a career or husband—preferably both. Meg is just another innocent who arrives in the big city, loses her luggage, and ends up in a women's hotel called The Nunnery. In this respect *Ask Any Girl* simply represents a modern verson of the small-town girl trying to make it in the big city, a plot that dates back to movies like *Morning Glory* (1933), *Stage Door* (1937), and *My Sister Eileen* (1942), films especially pegged for female audiences.

Meg claims she has come east to further her career rather than to capture a husband, but her job qualifications cast some doubt on this aspiration. As she later admits her qualifications for marriage are quite respectable: she's good-natured, fairly intelligent, and healthy—very healthy. She can cook and sew and, furthermore, her measurements are 34-24-34.

After keeping the wolves at bay at the Kampus Knits Co., Meg applies for a job as a field researcher. In a comic scene with David Niven (Miles Doughton), she coughs her way through her first cigarette test. Niven's seriousness serves as a perfect foil for MacLaine's nonchalance. With typical MacLaine candor, Meg readily admits she is a nonsmoker. Rejected as a suitable candidate, Meg lands the job from Miles's brother Evan, who is suitably impressed with her natural qualifications. Repeating his performance in *Teacher's Pet* (a Clarke Gable-Doris Day film), Gig Young (Evan) plays a bachelor whose hobby is collecting girls.

After several sequences depicting the ups and downs of field research (including being arrested in a brothel where Meg claims she was "just giving away samples"), Meg decides to concentrate on her second objective—getting a husband. Meanwhile, she has left The Nunnery and has moved in with a sexy roommate, Lisa, which according to Meg has all the disadvantages of marriage without any of its compensations. Like Ginny in *Some Came Run-*

Ask Any Girl—with Jim Backus.

Ask Any Girl—with Gig Young.

ning, Meg becomes a domesticated slave who does the shopping, cooking, and cleaning. These tasks are clearly portrayed as menial and are not sentimentalized as "the fun of keeping house."

In an effort to land Evan, Meg decides to use the subconscious weapons provided by motivational research. From this moment forward, the film resembles the long array of "how to" movies popular in the fifties and sixties (*How to Marry a Millionaire,* 1953; *How to Be Very, Very Popular,* 1955; *How to Stuff a Wild Bikini,* 1965), rather than the career-oriented films from the thirties mentioned earlier. Like other films of the period that supposedly taught women how to catch a man, the central action now shifts to MacLaine as aggressor instead of victim. With Miles's help, Meg sets about remodeling herself to attract Evan. Using Evan's little black book, Miles studies Evan's girlfriends "in the field" to learn their special secrets. Decked out with long earrings, false eye-

lashes, bright nail polish, and seductive perfume, Meg manages to hit Evan "below the level of his awareness." The experiment is an unqualified success. Miles is impressed with Meg's competence, which has grown in proportion to her intelligence and sophistication. Predictably, the two find they have more in common than a working relationship. Further, Meg has begun to question the whole effort to capture Evan. In one of the film's most significant lines Meg tells Miles, "I'm not an employee; I'm a piece of merchandise." At that moment Meg speaks for every woman who has ever tried to remodel herself to flatter a male fantasy.

Ask Any Girl exposes the destructiveness of viewing women as sexual objects as clearly as any film of the period. As Meg later realizes, she is no longer an individual but only a "composite" woman who possesses all of the fetishes that turn Evan on. When the hoped-for proposal finally comes, Meg justifiably turns him down, distressed at her own loss of identity. No longer willing to be guided by male expectations, Meg regains her former image and begins rethinking her whole moral code. She concludes that "the things girls are taught are nonsense" and decides the time has come to discard her virginity. Reflecting a sense of irony, she notes: "For centuries the women in her family settled for nothing less than marriage." Exactly where such sentiments might have led unfortunately remain unanswered. The subject of premarital sex is not seriously approached until *The Apartment*, made the following year. Hollywood's unwillingness to compromise the heroine necessitated the fairy-tale ending in which prince Miles saves princess Meg from the wolves. The retrogressive ending is pure Hollywood fun. Safe in the arms of Miles, Meg states, "I found who and what I'd been saving for—and that it was worth it too. If you don't believe me, ask any girl . . . woman."

Meg has become a woman alright, but not by virtue of her sexual initiation. If anything is clear from the film, it is the importance of holding to one's own identity. In that respect, *Ask Any Girl* becomes a moral allegory. The false Meg gets a false guy; the true Meg gets the real person. Like the screwball comedies, the *heroine* has managed to liberate the *hero* and turn him into a genuine human being.

The reviews of *Ask Any Girl* met with consensus. There were few words of praise for the routine plot, but all the critics were unanimous about the high performance of MacLaine. *Variety* claimed that she "gains increased stature as a performer and a personality with each new outing."[1] The reviewer also noted perceptively that MacLaine equally appealed to both sexes.

Penelope Houston, the English critic, went even further stating:

> But the film's main—and on the whole sufficient—justification is the presence of its star. Since Hitchcock's *The Trouble with Harry*, Miss MacLaine has been stealthily advancing on the position lately abandoned by Judy Holliday, as Hollywood's most calmly ingenuous comedy actress. Lacking Judy Holliday's wistful enjoyment of her own naiveté, she substitutes a combination of exaggerated innocence with almost ferociously exact timing.[2]

Clearly none of the critics took the film very seriously; but in hindsight, its relationship to MacLaine and to her later films cannot be overlooked. She herself stated later while filming *The Apartment*,

> In *Ask Any Girl*, what I was playing was situation comedy, and it was my second hardest part after this one. The actual comedy wasn't difficult, but when I dug down and asked myself what Meg Wheeler was all about, I didn't know because she was so close to me too.[3]

10

Career

Career (1959), MacLaine's fourth picture for Hal Wallis Productions, remains one of her least memorable films, despite the merits of the production as a whole. Although she received top female billing (preceding Carolyn Jones and newcomer Joan Blackman), her role is definitely minor. The part essentially falls into the category of supporting character actress, but without any of the special qualities that particularize the performance. The drunk scenes fail to qualify because they are not sufficiently idiosyncratic to create a lasting impression.

The film covers fourteen years in the life of Sam Lawson (Anthony Franciosa), an ambitious young actor from Lansing, Michigan, who comes to New York to establish his career. Together with another struggling artist, Maury Novak (Dean Martin), Sam forms a small off-Broadway company. Barbara, Sam's hometown sweetheart, joins him in New York for awhile but finally divorces him and returns home, unable to tolerate the endless poverty and hardship. Eventually, Maury gets a break and takes off for Hollywood. Increasingly bitter, Sam finds small parts and sympathy from a lonely theatrical agent, Shirley Drake (Carolyn Jones).

Maury, now a big Hollywood director, returns to New York to cast a new Broadway show. Sam, confident of his talent and friendship with Maury,

expects to get the lead. However, Maury rejects Sam as "unbankable," advising him to "wise up" or get out of acting. Livid with indignation, Sam determines to be a star at any cost.

Sam runs into Sharon Kensington (MacLaine), Maury's former girlfriend and the daughter of a successful Broadway producer, and he takes up where Maury left off. Sharon is rich, spoiled, and unhappy, and drowns her sorrows in a bottle. Seeing his chance to get ahead, Sam becomes Sharon's fourth husband.

One year later, Sharon, pregnant with Maury's child, comes to Sam for a divorce. Sam agrees on the condition he be given the lead in Maury's new play. During rehearsals, however, Maury and Kensington change the casting when they hear a big Hollywood star is interested in the part. Seething with anger, Sam threatens to kill Maury. Before anything further develops, Sam is sent to Korea. He returns during the House Un-American Affairs Committee Investigations. He supports himself as a waiter while waiting for his big break. Maury, now blacklisted for his early political associations, offers him a part in a new off-Broadway venture. At first, defensive, he turns him down but later changes his mind, encouraged by a chance meeting with his first wife, who claims now to understand his dedication and drive.

Maury's play proves a huge success and moves to

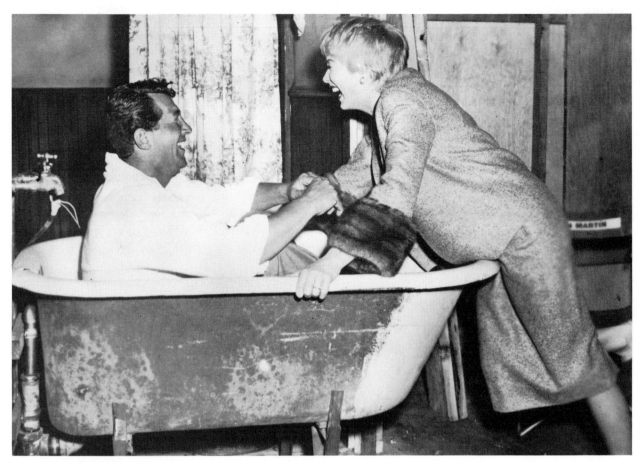

Career—with Dean Martin.

Career—with Anthony Franciosa and Joan Blackman.

Broadway. Before the curtain goes up, Shirley asks Sam whether all the suffering was worth it. Thinking for a moment, he answers, "Yes, it was worth it," and steps out to take his bow.

Although the story of the struggling artist was hardly a new subject, director Joseph Anthony handled the material with seriousness and a sense of naturalism that makes Sam's climb to the top a compelling story. Appropriately filmed in harsh black and white, the story focuses on dark, empty stages, gloomy back rooms, and dimly lit alleyways—the underside of Broadway and glittering marquees. Told in flashback from Sam's point of view, his cynicism seems visibly palpable. Yet, not every critic felt equally moved by this drama. One reviewer commented that Sam's chronic bad luck bordered on "masculine soap opera."

As Sharon Kensington, MacLaine appears as a girl with a loose tongue to match her loose morals. Decked out in a sexy black dress and short blond hair, Sharon spends most of the film in a drunken stupor—an extended version of the drunk scene in *Some Came Running*. Although she obviously knows the ropes of life in the big city, she is neither tough nor smart. Unable to stand on her own two feet, Sharon spends most of the film going from one protective situation to another, from one lover to the next. The movie also gives MacLaine ample opportunity to shriek and scream, sob and cry, laugh and giggle—three emotions that have become trademarks of all her later films.

Sharon does have one moment of truth. When she appeals to Sam for the divorce, she claims the right to love regardless of whether she has been "good" (a euphemism referring to her sexual behavior). Scorning the argument as advice from her psychiatrist, Sam remains unmoved. Even here Sharon is unable to persuasively affect the action.

Maury must step in to consummate the deal.

The last shot of Sharon occurs on the eve of Sam's success. Saddled with two children, Sharon has become sober, frumpy, and middleclass. Typifying the position of a married woman, she is not included in any of the action and is seen only in long shot. No longer a free agent or a useful tool, she has become a nonentity. Sharon Kensington is a complete washout compared with other MacLaine characters, past and future. She is weak and self-pitying, and does not even possess the dignity and self-determination that characterize prostitutes like Irma and, to a lesser degree, Ginny and Charity. Perhaps it is fitting, therefore, that in the end she just fades into the background.

11

Can-Can

MacLaine had now been in Hollywood for five years, yet not one of her films gave her the opportunity to utilize the specific talent that had earned her a Hollywood contract, namely, dancing. Her chance finally came, however, with the filming of *Can-Can* (1960), a Broadway musical with music by Cole Porter, story by Abe Burrows, and choreography by Michael Kidd. The film adaptation, directed by Walter Lang, was choreographed by Hermes Pan and starred MacLaine, Frank Sinatra, Maurice Chevalier, Louis Jourdan, and Juliet Prowse.

The story, set in the 1890s, concerns the romantic entanglements of Simone Pistache (MacLaine), a dancer and owner of the Cafe Le Bal Du Paradis; Francois Durnais (Sinatra), her lawyer and sometime lover; Paul Barriere (Chevalier), a fun-loving, gentle older judge; and Phillippe Forrestier (Jourdan), a crusading, younger member of the court who is determined to follow the letter of the law. Simone expends most of her energy fighting off gendarmes who are sent to close her cafe (the penalty for allowing performances of the can-can), and trying to convince Francois of the virtues of marriage.

Philippe comes to Montmartre to learn more about the immoral can-can, meets Simone, falls desperately in love, and proposes marriage. Simone is suspicious of his intentions at first, but she finally agrees to appear at a social event on board a Seine River boat. Seeking to embarass her in front of Philippe's upper crust friends, Francois convinces Simone to perform a rather vulgar song and dance. Simone breaks the engagement to Philippe, realizing that social differences will make marriage impossible, and instead decides to concentrate on making money. Angry at Francois for his indifference, surreptitiously she transfers ownership of the Cafe to Francois and readies her girls for a performance of the can-can. The police conduct a raid as expected, and Francois is taken off to jail. Slightly repentent, however, Simone fails to produce the paper that would condemn Francois.

Finally the judges decide to reevaluate the ban on the can-can and request a live performance of the dance. All agree, including the "ladies of the League," that the can-can is not offensive, and the film ends with Simone happily in the arms of Francois.

The movie was released in March 1960, to mixed reviews. Most critics were unmoved, and few could find justification for the expenditure of $6,000,000 on the extravagant Todd-AO musical. Most offense was leveled against MacLaine and Sinatra. Juxtaposed against Chevalier and Jourdan, their credibility as Frenchmen took a wide stretch

Can-Can

Can-Can—with Frank Sinatra.

Can-Can—with Juliet Prowse.

of the imagination. Many reviewers had vivid memories of the Francophile charms of *Gigi* only two years before (also starring Chevalier and Jourdan) and were disappointed. In contrast, *Can-Can* was a rather disjointed, raucous affair typified by flat performances from a group of rather distinctive personalities.

MacLaine's performance was particularly marred by a shrill voice and hysterical acting. Referring to MacLaine's voice, the critic Stanley Kauffmann once said, "she sounds like a Woolworth rejectee." As for the musical virtues of *Can-Can*, it may have possessed lavish sets and costumes, but the *New York Herald Tribune* summed it up best with its comment, "*Can-Can* does not represent any new level in musical comedy."[1] By 1960 the day of the big Hollywood musical was over. The great musicals of the fifties, beginning in 1951 with *Singin' in the Rain* and *An American in Paris* and including *Band Wagon* (1953), *Seven Brides for Seven Brothers* (1954), *Guys and Dolls* (1955), *Funny Face* (1957), and *Gigi* (1958), had run their course. After 1960 few musicals except those with a family orientation (e.g., *The Sound of Music*) found an audience; even the innovative *Sweet Charity* went unappreciated.

The main virtue of *Can-Can* was the dancing—unfortunately not MacLaine's. Next to the young Juliet Prowse, MacLaine looked clumsy and thick, especially dancing in ballet shoes in the Adam and Eve ballet. Bosley Crowther of *The New York Times* referred to her as "the foot-heavy Miss MacLaine." (MacLaine kept this review pasted to her mirror for months as preventive medicine against a swelled head). He felt even less disposed to her Apache dance, likening her to a beanbag being tossed about by several violent, young, male dancers. MacLaine herself recognized just how out of shape a dancer can become when she stops working out. She didn't make that mistake again when she took the dancing lead in *Sweet Charity*.

In fairness to MacLaine, however, she did compensate for her lack of physical adeptness with a high degree of spirit and élan. Her number "Come Along With Me" and the can-can finale were especially zesty.

The role of Simone has several similarities to Ginny in *Some Came Running* and also serves as a dry run for her much finer performance as Irma three years later. Like Ginny, Simone belongs to the lower social class and the sisterhood who make ends meet by serving men. Like her, too, Simone is soft in the middle and really wants to settle down with one man (in this respect she is like the other "sisters of the night" in *The Yellow Rolls Royce* and *Sweet Charity*). Like Ginny, Simone wants to be respected but somehow is always outclassed. Echoes of the comic drunk scene in *Some Came Running* appear in *Can-Can*—to be repeated again in *The Apartment* and *Ocean's Eleven*.

However, Simone is self-assured and aggressive. MacLaine has referred to her as "brazen" and "warm," a "real broad." What she lacks in class, she makes up for in sheer energy. The opening shot of Simone shows her, leg upon the table, in a pose assertively masculine and seductive at the same time. Simone is a living embodiment of the ambivalent attitudes toward women during the fifties. Though obviously a woman of experience, she is portrayed as excessively modest in one scene and lewdly vulgar in the next. MacLaine was the perfect actress for this era, in that she infused even the most trashy dames with an aura of niceness, combining sex and goodness in one character. It is significant that often what attracts men to MacLaine characters—her vivaciousness and unrestrained extroversion—becomes the reason they reject her later. Independent by nature, she accepts a back seat the minute love enters the picture.

Only in the Adam and Eve ballet does Simone have an opportunity to vent her angry feelings. Dressed as Eve in a tight-fitting, gold lamé bodysuit, Simone not only proves that sin was not invented in Monmartre but also has a chance to take her knocks at the male species. The ballet concludes with Eve delivering a direct hit to Adam's jaw. Sensual as the whole may be, the ballet is regrettably jarring stylistically and badly conceived balletically.

Unintentionally, *Can-Can* received some unexpected publicity. As part of his 1959 visit to the

Publicity shot from *Can-Can*.

On the set of *Can-Can* with husband Steve Parker.

United States, Nikita Khrushchev was taken to the 20th Century lot during the shooting of *Can-Can*. MacLaine and Sinatra were asked to act as host and hostess. Sinatra appropriately sang "Live and Let Live" from the film, and MacLaine gave a prepared speech in Russian, which she had memorized phonetically. According to MacLaine, Khrushchev was extremely cordial and seemed to enjoy himself thoroughly. Only later did she learn that this was perhaps not the case. When asked to comment on his impression of Hollywood, Khrushchev replied, "Immoral .... The face of humanity is more beautiful than its backside." In anger MacLaine quipped, "I think he's upset we wore panties."[2]

Khrushchev obviously harbored no ill feelings towards MacLaine and continued to take an interest in her career. A year and a half later MacLaine received the following message (delivered through Khrushchev's interpreter): "The Premier sends his regards, wishes to be remembered to you, and says he's just seen your new picture, *The Apartment*, and you've improved."[3]

12

The Apartment

The highlight of MacLaine's early career is clearly her performance as Fran Kubelik in *The Apartment*, released May 1960. Although *Some Came Running* had catapulted her to stardom and brought her offers of all kinds, it was not until *The Apartment* that she had an opportunity to work with a demanding director like Billy Wilder, who could exert the necessary discipline to hone her spontaneous style, eliminate her cute mannerisms, which were already becoming tiresome, and accentuate her ability to play both comedy and drama.

Written by the team of Billy Wilder and I.A.L. Diamond, who had previously scored successes together with *Love in the Afternoon* (1957) and *Some Like It Hot* (1959), *The Apartment* has been designated by critic Hollis Alpert as "a dirty fairy tale, with a shnook for a hero, and a sad little elevator operator for a fairy princess,"[1] Alpert is not far from the mark. The story chronicles the rise to success of an ambitious, young IBM operator who aspires to become an executive. Realizing that favors hasten advancement, he has begun lending the key to his bachelor apartment to several executives who are currently involved in extramarital affairs. As played by Jack Lemmon, C. C. Baxter is not a Machiavellian manipulator who knows how to play one prince off against another, but rather the classic little man who is used by the system because he is not clever enough to gain the upper hand. The opening office scenes with rows of identical desks reminds one of King Vidor's *The Crowd*. Shut out of his own apartment, Baxter spends many an evening asleep on a park bench.

In the role of Fran Kubelik, MacLaine has her first chance to play an ordinary working girl, a switch from Hindu princesses, dipsomaniacs, cowgirls, and madams. Initially, Fran appears good-natured and cheerful, as she puts a rose in Baxter's lapel, wishes him "good luck," and "blasts off" in her elevator. However, it soon becomes apparent that her merry exterior masks considerable unhappiness. In the following scenes, her sunny personality quickly dissolves, as do her pert good looks. The cause is clear—J. D. Sheldrake (Fred MacMurray), the company's top executive. As Fran herself admits, "It's hell going with a married man."

Moving up another rung on the ladder of success, he is distressed to discover that the girl Sheldrake has been taking to his apartment is none other than Fran, the girl he had fancied for himself. Worse still is the knowledge that Sheldrake confides to Baxter that he has no intention of changing his present marital status.

All proceeds apace until Christmas Eve when

The Apartment—with Naomi Stevens.

Baxter returns to his apartment to discover Fran sprawled out on his bed, unconscious from an overdose of sleeping pills. With the help of his neighbor, Dr. Dreyfuss, the two men walk Fran back and forth for the rest of the evening, as the sympathetic doctor mockingly suggests he should "charge by the mile." The scene is typically Wilderian—a perfect blend of comedy and tragedy made more poignant by Dr. Dreyfuss's assumption that Baxter is the rake responsible for the near fatality.

As Fran recovers, nourished on Mrs. Dreyfuss's chicken soup and spaghetti (which Baxter strains through his tennis racket in an unforgettable scene), the two exchange confidences and play gin rummy (an injoke that Wilder added to the script because of MacLaine's fondness for the game).

When Sheldrake, abandoned by his recently informed wife, decides to marry Fran, Baxter finally takes a stand and returns the key to the executive washroom, telling Sheldrake he has decided to become "a mensh" as Dr. Dreyfuss advised.

That night, New Year's Eve, Fran also asserts herself for the first time and rushes back to the apartment. Momentarily frightened by a sound that she mistakes for a gun shot, she bursts in to find Baxter opening a bottle of champagne. Baxter declares his love, but the last line belongs to Fran, who merely responds, "Shut up and deal."

Although some critics had reservations about Wilder's cynicism and especially his lapses into sentimentality, *The Apartment* won the Academy Award for the best picture of the year, with little competition from *The Alamo, Elmer Gantry, Sons and Lovers,* and *The Sundowners.* In addition, MacLaine, Jack Lemmon, and Jack Kruschen (Dr. Dreyfuss) were all nominated for Oscars and Wilder walked off with two awards—one for best director, the other for the best original screenplay. (Mac-

The Apartment—with Jack Lemmon.

The Apartment—with Jack Lemmon.

Laine was nominated as best actress but lost out to Elizabeth Taylor in *Butterfield 8*. She did, however, receive an award at the Venice Film Festival). Such enthusiasm was no doubt prompted by the real desire on the part of producers and audiences alike for adult entertainment with some semblance to the facts of life. By 1960 the sugar-coated conservatism that had marked the films of the McCarthy era was beginning to seem mawkish and out-of-step with reality. Films from Europe like *Hiroshima, Mon Amour, Lady Chatterley's Lover,* and *Room at the Top* (all released in the United States in 1959) dealt with the complexity of adult sexual relationships and reminded filmgoers that movies could provide more than a mere means of escape. *The Apartment* clearly seemed like a breath of fresh air, despite the plot manipulations and the conventional happy ending. It was a happy combination of two elements: down-to-earth characters and an entertaining plot, with some barbs at big business for good measure .

The most important aspect of *The Apartment,* however, was not its bitter revelations into the men's world of success, but rather its insights into the plight of the average, urban, single female whose life contains neither career nor marriage. Prior to the sixties, heroines were either safely married or pursuing a successful career. Each had her appropriate mode of behavior. Wives were supposed to be decent, asexual, understanding, and supportive of the men in their lives. Career women were aggressive, slightly masculine, intelligent, and independent—women who didn't need a man until the last reel. Women who slept with men outside of marriage were tramps, vamps, or tarts, and paid for it in the end. Fran Kubelik fits into none of these categories. Despite her sexual permissiveness, she is basically a nice girl—a babe in the woods among New York wolves. Marjorie Rosen has pointed out that Fran is "not particularly freer than her chaste compatriots, she is more stupid—a victim of loneliness and naïveté."[2] Whereas loose women of the

With Jack Lemmon

hero's and sometimes ours as well). Thus, heroines could have their fun and remain unblemished at the same time. Such heroines have come to be called good-bad girls—who appear to be bad, but who are in reality good (i.e., sexually pure).

In *The Apartment*, Fran becomes one of the first really bad girls (albeit with a heart of gold) to get her man, certainly a major breakthrough for the time. She does not get off scot-free, however; her unsuccessful suicide serves as due punishment, providing the one unbelievable note in an otherwise believable film. Ironically it is not the would-be sinner (Fran) who is rehabilitated at the end, but Baxter. Although he probably doesn't fully comprehend the true meaning of "being a mensh," but by turning in his executive key he opts for human values over monetary ones. In the end, they have saved each other, and together they can drop out of the ranks of those who "get took."

Wilder was delighted with MacLaine's performance in *The Apartment*. Shortly after its release he commented:

> What she did in that picture was amazing. She came to us with that kind of offhand, one-take manner that The Rat Pack has adopted as its working habit. I was worried. I thought she wasn't serious. But when she saw how I work, she soon caught on and was willing to work hard on every movement and every line. . . . . She is a remarkable girl. I believe she is going to last a long time.[3]

He added later, "I feel we've only scratched the surface. She's enormously talented, and she gets better all the time."[4]

Jack Lemmon was equally taken with MacLaine. In an interview he said, "She's very free in front of a camera. . . . . She doesn't care how she's going to look on the screen. She just plays the part and you always get the feeling, 'Look, I've been there, Charlie, I know.' "[5]

movies slept with men for ulterior motives (money, ambition, power, lust), Fran sleeps with Sheldrake because she loves him. Sex is one way in which she demonstrates this love.

Perhaps the real innovation of *The Apartment* can best be seen by Wilder's handling of the ending. Prior to 1960, a screen heroine who participated in premarital sex became automatically ineligible to win the hero. She was conveniently eliminated (by stray arrows, bullets, or unforseen accidents) like Ginny in *Some Came Running*. Where such manipulations were unbelievable or unacceptable, plots were stretched out of shape to prove that the seeming indiscretion of the heroine was in truth a misunderstanding (the

13

Ocean's Eleven

Following *Can-Can*, Frank Sinatra embarked on a venture for his own production company (Dorchester Productions) entitled *Ocean's Eleven*. Heading a cast that included Dean Martin, Sammy Davis, Jr., Peter Lawford, Angie Dickinson, Richard Conte, Cesar Romero, Joey Bishop, and Akim Tamiroff, Sinatra and members of The Clan romped through a two-hour comic caper in which everyone had a chance to impersonate himself.

Filmed in Las Vegas, the plot centers on the efforts of eleven wartime buddies to simultaneously hit five, big hotel casinos at midnight on New Year's Eve. In addition to the stellar cast, *Ocean's Eleven* also utilized the talents of several Hollywood celebrities in cameo roles. On the roster were George Raft, Red Skelton, Ilka Chase, Buddy Lester, Henry Silva, and, of course, Shirley MacLaine. MacLaine agreed to appear as a drunken dame, a part she had perfected in previous pictures.

The film is full of injokes, tongue-in-cheek comments, and double entendres. MacLaine's scene characterizes the entire movie.

As Sam Harmon (Martin) makes final preparations at the Sahara Hotel, two floozies pull up in an automobile. Dead drunk, MacLaine emerges from the car in a blue silk dress and a white fur stole. When she leans over to find a key she has accidently dropped, she can hardly get up again. Hoping to hurry her along, Martin attempts to help. In a gesture reminiscent of *Artists and Models*, MacLaine grabs Martin and pins him down with a kiss. Then, in typical MacLaine fashion, she giggles. Her mood changes, however, when she realizes he wants her out of the way. "It's a dirty deal," she claims. "I don't fit into your picture, huh?" Martin replies, "From here on in you don't, sweetheart." Unruffled she retorts, "It so happens, I'm very much in demand."

14

All in a Night's Work

All in a Night's Work (1961), a Hal Wallis Production directed by Joseph Anthony, repeats many of the characters and situations that occur in earlier MacLaine films. The plot is one extended double entendre, which arises from an initial misunderstanding between stars Dean Martin and MacLaine.

As Tony Ryder, Martin impersonates a handsome playboy who, upon the death of his uncle, inherits Ryder and Company, a major Manhattan publishing company. Ryder also learns that his uncle kept a girlfriend who was with him when he died in a Palm Beach hotel room and who is likely to demand blackmail in the near future. A detective hands Ryder an earring belonging to the mystery woman. The earring forms the Chinese character for "good."

Convening his first company meeting to settle a dispute between management and labor, Ryder instantly notices the single, matching earring on an intelligent, attractive, young researcher, Katie Robbins (MacLaine). In an effort to meet the enemy head on, Ryder takes Katie to lunch to discuss business. Meanwhile, he hires Detective O'Hara to tail her.

O'Hara reports on Katie's attempt to return an $11,000 mink coat to a fancy fur salon. He concludes that Katie is their woman. We learn, however, that Katie obtained the coat as a reward for saving a drowning millionaire (Mr. Hackett) while on her vacation in Florida. Katie, suspicious of his ultimate desires, decides to return the coat or pay for it herself. We also learn that after the rescue Katie took off her soaking clothing and dashed from Hackett's room, clad solely in a bath towel. She ran through the elder Ryder's room, where she stumbled and lost her earring (while he lay already dead on the bed), and then fled the hotel.

Subsequent conversations with Katie (always at cross purposes) convince Ryder that she is out to take him for all he is worth. In an effort to pacify her, Ryder gives Katie a $200 raise, which naturally baffles her. O'Hara recommends that they try marrying her off and then attempt counterblackmail.

Conveniently Katie is already engaged. Her fiancé is a stuffy straitlaced veterinarian, Warren Kingsley, Jr. (Cliff Robertson). But, Katie ruins her chances of marriage by making a poor impression on Warren's conservative parents. Making one blunder after another, she proceeds to get drunk and ends by dancing the cha-cha with the cook in a fancy restaurant. The engagement is immediately called off.

Misunderstanding Katie's refusal to accept the

All in a Night's Work

$200 raise, Ryder invites her to his apartment for another business meeting. Once inside his bedroom, he tries to soften her up with romantic lighting and tender words. Katie takes the whole thing as a joke and rattles off stories of former conquests. When she finally realizes that Ryder is taking her seriously, she turns to Warren (who has had a change of heart) for protection. But Warren is easily put off again by a tape recording of Katie's so-called "true confession." When the real truth emerges, Katie's good name is once more established. Acknowledging his own true feelings for Katie, Ryder closes the film with a kiss.

In many ways *All in a Night's Work* functions as a companion piece to *Ask Any Girl*. Once again the major characters form a romantic triangle composed of a young, innocent working girl and two men—one a fun-loving lady's man, the other a serious professional. In both films MacLaine manages to introduce chaos into the ordered lives of the bores, eventually liberating them from the

restrictive bounds of conventionality. A similar triangle exists in *Can-Can* (with identical results), although Simone differs considerably from the innocent Meg Wheeler and the moral Katie Robbins. The major difference between *All in a Night's Work* and *Ask Any Girl* lies in the outcome. In *All in a Night's Work* the heroine falls for the playboy; in *Ask Any Girl* she rejects him.

The character of Katie shares much in common with Meg Wheeler. In addition to their jobs as Manhattan corporation employees, both show a strange mixture of intelligence and naïveté. Both fluctuate between being engagingly open and awkwardly self-conscious. Dressed alike in proper, tailored suits (which never quite hide MacLaine's physical assets), they both lead exemplary, virtuous lives. MacLaine utilizes the same mannerisms in both portrayals—the raised eyebrow, the smirking mouth, the quizzical look, the soft giggle, and shoulders that rise and fall with every laugh.

Both young ladies go to inordinate lengths to

All in a Night's Work—with Dean Martin

All in a Night's Work

protect their reputation. Meg gives up her job at Kampus Knits to avoid the sexual advances of Mr. Maxwell. Katie dashes out of Hackett's bedroom and, later in a comic scene, insists on paying for the mink coat herself rather than accepting his gift. (At the rate of $5.00 per week, this will take her forty-five years.)

The scene with Warren's parents is analogous to Meg's interview with Miles Doughton. In both instances, MacLaine's candor and clumsiness are perfect foils for the stuffy mannerisms and control of the opposition. Stressing gesture over verbal wit, MacLaine's behavior borders on traditional slapstick comedy.

Like *Ask Any Girl*, *All in a Night's Work* resounds with racy double entendres (including the title). One in particular occurs at the first business meeting, when it is suggested that Ryder and Katie get together to "feel each other out." Such humor, typical of the late fifties, reflects a strain against the restrictive production code of the day.

Unlike Meg, who spends the first half of *Ask Any Girl* responding to acts of aggression, Katie is an active agent whose decisiveness matches her morals. Having rescued Hackett, paid for the fur coat, refused the $200 raise, it is hardly surprising that she calls the shots in the romantic realm. Turning to Ryder she says, "You can kiss me if you like."

The character of Katie is modeled on the good-bad girl referred to earlier (see *The Apartment*). Although Katie's true character, like the earring that symbolizes "good," is revealed to viewers early in the film, Ryder does not become cognizant of the facts until the final moments. The discrepancy between our knowledge and his provides the basic humor of the work.

And, of course, the film would not be complete without the prerequisite drunk and crying scenes that crop up in every MacLaine movie.

The film was released in March 1961. The reviews followed a typical pattern—lukewarm responses to the film, high praise for MacLaine's performance. Oddly enough, no critic questioned MacLaine's selection of roles or recommended better vehicles. *Variety* did note that

Miss MacLaine is still playing the sweet, naïve, tangle-footed kook she began a few years back in *Some Came Running*, but she plays it with such innocent sincerity and comic gusto that she thoroughly succeeds in winning over the audiences and gives the film a much-needed shot in the funny-bone.[1]

All in a Night's Work—with Cliff Robertson and Charlie
Ruggles.

15

Two Loves

Two Loves (1961) was MacLaine's fourteenth picture since 1955. Except for 1957, she was averaging two films a year—perhaps not as impressive as Bette Davis's early career (a record forty-one films in eight years: 1932-1939), but by 1950s standards it represented sustained hard work. Like *Some Came Running* and *The Apartment*, *Two Loves* was a step in a new direction, although the film was neither a critical nor a financial success.

The story of *Two Loves* (entitled *Spinster* in England) is based on a novel by Sylvia Ashton-Warner and deals with the life of an American schoolteacher living in a remote part of New Zealand. Dedicated to bridging the gap between Maori customs and Western education, Anna Vorontosov (MacLaine) finds herself in constant opposition to the formality of the British system. She is adored by her students and also finds unexpected support from the new English school inspector, Abercrombie (Jack Hawkins). Abercrombie not only appreciates the value of Anna's unorthodox methods but also finds her a remarkable woman.

In addition to Abercrombie, Anna has attracted the attention of Paul Lathrope (Laurence Harvey), an unhappy, neurotic, and sometimes childish fellow teacher. Although Anna finds Paul interesting, her sexual inhibitions prevent her from responding to his sexual advances.

Despite her liberal notions on education, Anna is shocked to learn of the pregnancy of her charming, fifteen-year-old assistant, Whareparita (Nobu McCarthy). She finds it difficult to understand the community's casual acceptance of Whareparita's unborn baby, whose father refuses to be recognized. Whareparita subsequently miscarries, but the event forces Anna to question her own moral standards. She concludes that perhaps she is the child, and Whareparita the adult.

Following a tense evening in which Paul ardently declares his love, Anna abruptly sends him away. The next day she learns he has been killed in a motorcycle accident during the night. Anna blames herself, believing that Paul's death was possibly suicidal. At Paul's funeral she discovers that he was the father of Whareparita's child.

Anna is consoled by Abercrombie who assures her that no one is really responsible for another's fate. He also tells her of his plans to divorce his wife. After spending the night together, Anna and Abercrombie arrive at school, both aglow from the blossom of their new love.

The film, released May 1961, pleased no one. MacLaine referred to it as "an unfortunate film." She had herself chosen the script to fulfill a contract commitment with MGM but evidently had some reservations about the project from the start.

The reviews were devastating on every level.

Two Loves—as a schoolteacher.

Films in Review wrote: "This film is so bad cinematically, and so reprehensible sociologically, that MGM has not known what to do with it."[1] None of the actors received praise, including MacLaine. *The N.Y. Herald Tribune* said, "Miss MacLaine looked decidedly uncomfortable in a role with which one doubts she could feel any compatibility. A part of her characterization clearly works against the impression of disturbed prudery the characterization means to establish."[2] Even the sets were criticized. *Time* referred to the "artsy-craftsy exotica of Trader Vics."[3] Most of the critics felt the main problem lay with Ben Maddow's screenplay and his failure to provide depth and motivation to the central characters. Much of the blame obviously belongs to Charles Walters, a director best known for his musicals, but who had also directed MacLaine in the comedy *Ask Any Girl.*

Two Loves—with Laurence Harvey

Two Loves

But despite all of the limitations, the picture provided MacLaine with her first role as a totally intelligent, self-sufficient woman, who spends her life doing something more constructive than being an elevator operator, a high-class secretary, or a whore. In this respect it was MacLaine's first role as a liberated woman. It is too bad that the producers felt it necessary to introduce such a maudlin love story to spice up the narrative. No doubt they believed that the story of an innovative, dedicated schoolteacher would lack sufficient interest to carry the film. Oddly enough, the only memorable scenes in an otherwise slow-moving, melodramatic movie are the episodes in the classroom.

More offensive and revealing was the implicit assumption that an unmarried woman who found her work and life totally fulfilling was obviously sublimating. The basic contradiction between Anna's liberated life-style and teaching methods and her reactionary sexual morality never seems believable. *Variety,* sensitive to this point, stated that

> she (MacLaine) is presented as a self-sufficient woman seemingly quite content to thrust herself into her work. Yet the story is bent on proving that she is an unhappy, incomplete woman. Unfortunately, it attempts to do so by offering her a choice of males who would not necessarily tempt even a woman of easy virtue. Frigidity is a serious problem tackled here as if it can be erased by one night with a man.[4]

The necessity of treating unmarried women as incomplete, and the enforced happy ending (the loss of Anna's virginity), are a throwback to films of the thirties and forties that implied that all a woman really needed was a good man.

Haskell has written, "A woman's work is almost always seen as provisional, and almost never as a lifelong commitment, or as part of her definition as a woman."[5] Pictures starring Katharine Hepburn, Irene Dunne, Jean Arthur, and Ginger Rogers portrayed successful career women who only really made it when they could prove their competence in the bedroom or the kitchen.

As Anna Vorontosov, MacLaine appears with long red hair, creating a contrast to her earlier pixie images. She seems slightly older than in previous films, dressed in frumpy clothes that look as if she were rehearsing for *The Children's Hour* (a reflection of Hollywood's concept of the schoolteacher). Despite Anna's strict moral code, she demonstrates many of the qualities that have come to be associated with MacLaine: openness, vitality, and a casual manner. The quality that first attracts her to Paul is her frankness. One of the most delightful moments in the film is Anna's animated rendition of the Maori story of Pogo. Although she nips some from the bottle that she hides in her tea caddy, *Two Loves* is one film that avoids the ubiquitous drunk scene. We are not likewise spared the sight of tears. Anna has a good cry before Abercrombie comes to rescue her.

The disaster of *Two Loves* was not a complete waste. The film turned MacLaine in a new direction. The next several films (*My Geisha, The Children's Hour, Two for the Seesaw,* and *Irma la Douce*) all depicted women of some substance and depth, whose independent initiative overrode their personal and professional problems. Before undertaking a series of routine comedies in the mid-sixties, MacLaine created four memorable female portraits that were unequaled until her role in *Sweet Charity* in 1968.

16

My Geisha

Following *Two Loves*, MacLaine took Sachi, then age three, to Japan to film *My Geisha*. The film was very special to the Parker household for two reasons: one, it was their first joint production—a film starring Shirley MacLaine and produced by Steve Parker under the banner of Sachiko Productions (later they joined forces again on *John Goldfarb, Please Come Home)*; two, the original scenario, written by veteran screenwriter Norman Krasna, was based on semibiographical material strongly paralleling the lives of Shirley and Steve.

My Geisha is a romantic comedy about the life and career of Lucy Dell (MacLaine), a top-ranking Hollywood comedienne, and her husband Paul Robaix (Yves Montand), a successful screen director. Paul, determined to switch from comedy to drama, has his heart set on a film version of *Madam Butterfly*. Lucy professes great interest in the role of Cho-Cho-San, but Paul feels she is not right for the part. For this project he wants an authentic Japanese actress and real locations in Japan.

After Paul leaves for Japan with Robert Moore (Bob Cummings), Lucy's frequent co-star, Lucy learns that the studio is unwilling to put up the entire funding without her name on the credits as a guaranteed draw. Motivated by a genuine desire to help Paul and by a need to prove she can play the part, Lucy convinces their friend and producer Sam Lewis (Edward G. Robinson) to take her to Tokyo where she hopes to change Paul's mind.

As a surprise, Lucy dresses as a geisha and joins the evening festivities at the local geisha house where Paul and Robert are being entertained. Lucy is so convincing in her impersonation that Paul does not recognize her. In fact, the next day, unable to find the right leading lady, he decides to screen test Lucy, who now goes under the name of Yoko Mori.

Although Sam is against the deception, Lucy procedes with the screen test. Wearing a traditional wig and kimono, special makeup, and contact lenses that change her eyes from blue to brown, Lucy passes the test. Paul is particularly taken with her modesty and old-fashioned ideas. Not surprisingly, he also finds she has a remarkable ability to perform naturally before the camera.

To prepare herself properly for the film, Lucy moves into a Japanese hotel, where her constant companion and teacher Kazumi Ito (Yoko Tani) schools her in the art of being a geisha. As filming progresses, Robert falls desperately in love with Yoko and persuades Paul to propose to Yoko in his name. During their evening together, Paul confesses to Yoko his need to succeed on his own—not as his wife's director. For the first time Lucy understands how much this project means to Paul.

My Geisha—with Yves Montand.

When shooting is almost ended, Paul accidently discovers the truth while watching a negative print of the film. The negative reverses colors and exposes Lucy's blue eyes. Angry and hurt, he decides to leave Lucy after the film is completed, but not before attempting to seduce Yoko to make Lucy believe he is unfaithful. Feeling betrayed, Lucy performs the hara-kiri scene with genuine feelings of despair.

On opening night, Kazumi gives Lucy a fan that reads, "Nothing before you, oh my husband." Overcoming her pride, Lucy joins Paul onstage and announces that Yoko Mori, as previously planned, has entered a convent and cannot be with them. With new understanding, Paul and Lucy clasp hands and bow as Paul receives the applause for his new success.

The film's biographical references were apparent to anyone who knew the slightest bit about the Parker's family life. As Lucy Dell, Hollywood's biggest box-office star, MacLaine was right on target. In 1962 MacLaine was still under contract to Hal Wallis and was not earning top dollars (her free-lance deals on *Can-Can* and *The Apartment* were a different story). By the time she filmed *Irma la Douce* the following year, however, she was pulling in $800,000 per film, which certainly qualified her as one of the biggest stars on the screen. (Lucy Dell can also be associated with comic actress Lucille Ball).

Paul Robaix, the other half of the creative duo, had obvious parallels with Steve Parker, who in real life was as talented a producer as Paul is a director. Like Paul, Steve had great fears about becoming Mr. MacLaine. The setting of *My Geisha* was a natural for Parker and provided him an oppor-

My Geisha—with Yoko Tani.

My Geisha—with Yves Montand.

tunity to capture on film his love and respect for the island country.

In addition to the characters and setting, *My Geisha* also incorporated small details that coincided with actual fact. MacLaine did indeed have special training for the role of Lucy/Yoko. For two weeks she resided at the famed Gion Caburenjo (a geisha training school), learning the traditional arts practiced by all accomplished geisha—music, dance, and the tea ceremony. According to MacLaine, "No Westerner had ever been allowed into such a training school, much less lived there."[1] Although MacLaine was unusually tall for a typical geisha, she mastered sitting gracefully, walking with toes in and knees down, the proper use of her hands, how to flutter a fan, and other qualities deemed admirable by Japanese men.

Also as depicted in *My Geisha,* Parker hired a Japanese cameraman, who was responsible for the much praised visual beauty of the work.

However, despite MacLaine's field work and the appeal of watching movie stars making a movie, the critics were not taken with the film. None of the reviewers exactly disliked the film (all conceded it was entertaining), but most felt that the transparent plot based on an elaborate case of mistaken identity eventually wore thin. But Krasna, who had based a good part of his thirty-year career developing this theme (in both comedy and drama), certainly gave the situation a couple of new twists. Also, critics felt that Yves Montand was weak in the role and failed to exhibit the charisma that had made him a star in the European cinema.

MacLaine did not seem to be affected by the negative comments and was generally pleased with the film. Referring to English director Jack Cardiff's first comic effort, she said, "Jack has a wonderful sense of pace."

She added: "Comedy's a very fleeting thing, it's something so vague it's like gossamer, you can't tell a person how to be funny or how to make an audience laugh. Even a director cannot be certain of physical things that will make an audience laugh, or visual things."[2]

But *My Geisha* is more than a comedy. Seldom has a comedy had such a touching ending. To what degree this scene coincided with fact will only be known by a few, but the love generated by the two fictional characters was no doubt reflective of the real MacLaine-Parker relationship. MacLaine pointed out: "On paper the script, which Norman

My Geisha

Krasna wrote, looks like a comedy; but in the development of the shooting we found an underlying theme which is absolutely realistic."[3]

My Geisha gave MacLaine another opportunity to play both serious and comic roles, and she switched effortlessly back and forth between the two (witness the moving scene with Montand in which she discovers her husband's true feelings followed by her comic antics as she tries to evade Robert's hot pursuit). The film is also MacLaine's first portrayal of two personalities. Earlier roles revealed incipient characteristics, but *My Geisha* is the first film to develop this theme fully.

As Lucy/Yoko, MacLaine embodies two very different concepts of womanhood—each arising from a specific culture. Lucy, educated on the value of American ingenuity, is ambitious, aggressive, hard working, unrestrained, sometimes frivolous, and competitive with men—much like MacLaine herself. In contrast, Yoko is reserved and modest, putting the needs of others, particularly men, before her own.

Obviously, both patterns have their limitations. Neither extreme seems appropriate to a happy married life by contemporary standards. It is understandable that American audiences would find Yoko charming, although hardly suitable as a model for American women. Even in Japan older notions concerning a woman's place are dying out—much to Paul's remorse. On the other hand, Lucy, along with her truly admirable qualities, suffers from an inability to appreciate that the very things that mean so much to her are equally important to Paul, not as a man, but as a person. This is what Lucy learns.

What is particularly noteworthy about *My Geisha* is that Lucy learns her lesson herself; it is not imposed on her through humiliation. Further, by learning to give, she grows as a human being. This happens not in the traditional manner where suffering and sacrifice equaled womanhood, but by allowing Paul to maintain his dignity. Lucy does, after all, act from a position of strength. Ultimately, she has not damaged her career. If anything, she has proved to herself (and to Paul) her ability to handle a new dramatic range. It is refreshing to see a female character with such power and success who still possesses all of the feminine virtues. One does wonder if the roles had been reversed whether Paul would have helped to boost Lucy's career ambitions and whether she would have planned to leave him. But, putting aside these questions, we are left with the impression that Lucy and Paul have reached a new plateau built on true equality and mutual respect.

17

The Children's Hour

In 1961 when William Wyler and the Mirisch brothers decided to film Lillian Hellman's 1934 play about lesbianism, the idea seemed very daring. In terms of movie history it was. *The Children's Hour* was the first American film to deal openly with the question of lesbianism. William Wyler also directed an earlier film adaptation—*These Three*—in 1936, but the lesbian relationship had been cautiously converted into a story of adultery. By 1962, however, public sophistication had come a long way. Most critics found the community outrage against the two accused schoolteachers hard to buy, indicating the gap between film production and general consumption.

The drama focuses on Karen Wright (Audrey Hepburn) and Martha Dobie (MacLaine), two women in their twenties who run a boarding school for young girls. The two women, close friends since college, share responsibilities for teaching and housekeeping. Karen, after a two-year engagement, finally decides to marry her patient fiancé, Dr. Joseph Carter (James Garner). On hearing the news, Martha angrily accuses Karen of deserting her just as the school is getting on its feet. Martha's Aunt Lily (Miriam Hopkins), who has raised her from childhood, tells Martha she is jealous by nature and that her feelings for Karen are "unnatural."

This conversation is overheard by a malicious twelve-year-old, Mary Tilford (Karen Balkin), who makes a practice of eavesdropping, lying, and temper tantrums. Although she does not fully comprehend Aunt Lily's accusations, she stores the knowledge to be used later against the two teachers. Earlier, Karen had caught Mary in an obvious lie, which Mary obstinately denied, and had taken disciplinary action. Mary has been spoiled by her wealthy grandmother, Mrs. Amelia Tilford (Fay Bainter), and she balks at any restraint on her wishes.

Acting on her malice, Mary tells her grandmother what she has heard, embellishing it with lies gleaned from forbidden fiction she secretly reads at night. Mrs. Tilford, convinced of Mary's veracity, immediately withdraws Mary from the school and informs the other parents, who do likewise. When Karen and Martha discover the ugly rumor, they openly challenge Mrs. Tilford. Mary and her friend Rosalie (who fears Mary's retribution) are questioned, but both children stick to their original story.

After losing a much publicized lawsuit against Mrs. Tilford (primarily based on Aunt Lily's refusal to appear as a character witness), Karen sends Joe away. She senses a change in his feelings and refuses to jeopardize his happiness and future success by asking for his continued loyalty. Convinced that Joe will never return, Karen suggests

The Children's Hour—with Audrey Hepburn and Karen
Balkin.

that she and Martha go elsewhere to make a new
life for themselves.

In a long monologue, Martha admits her feelings
of love for Karen, which she fears come close to
the vicious rumors. Confused and unhappy, she
breaks down in tears. The unexpected visit and
apology of Mrs. Tilford, belatedly aware of the real
truth, does little to alter the situation.

The film ends with Martha's suicide and funeral.
Filled with self-hatred, she was unable to bear her
sense of guilt. At the funeral Karen stands alone.
Dignified and confident, she walks past all those
who sought to hurt her, her head held high.

Reviews for the *Children's Hour* (released as *The
Loudest Whisper* in England) ran the gamut of
critical possibilities. Writing for *The New York
Times,* Bosley Crowther stated, "There is nothing
about this picture of which he (Wyler) can be very
proud."[1] Two days before, *Variety* referred to
"the general excellence of Wyler's production."
The critics also varied in their evaluation of
MacLaine's performance. *Films in Review* called

MacLaine "incompetent" in the role of Martha,
and Crowther wrote that she "inclines to be too
kittenish in some scenes and do too much vocal
hand-wringing toward the end."[2] On the other
hand, *Time* said, "Shirley MacLaine, all forlorn,
gives the best performance . . . . She gives viewers a
touching and indelible lesson in what cinema acting
is all about.[3] Paul V. Beckley echoed similar sentiments in *The N. Y. Herald Tribune,* claiming,

> What makes Miss MacLaine's performance so much
> more trenchant is that while Miss Hepburn is asked to
> portray little more than disbelief, defiance and the
> posture of pride, Miss MacLaine is absolutely in-
> volved. Her scene of horrible and fatal self-reproach is
> the most affecting psychological event in the picture
> and its dramatic high point.[4]

As the first American film to broach the subject
of lesbianism (the French had treated it in *Olivia,*
1950, and in *The Girl with the Golden Eyes,*
1960), the film is timid, completely avoiding even
a mention of the word. However, though the work
does not have the explicitness of later films

(particularly *Therese and Isabelle*, 1968, and *The Killing of Sister George*, 1969), its very suggestiveness (an element that Wyler develops visually, as well) speaks more broadly of a universal, latent capacity in all women.

Joan Mellen points out quite correctly in her essay "Lesbianism in the Movies" that the main focus of the film is not on psychology but on sociology, "showing the intolerance of a puritanical, self-righteous community which would drive a woman to death for her sexual preferences."[5] This focus typifies the original text as well. In no way is *The Children's Hour* a defense of lesbianism; rather, it is a study of the destructive forces that can act upon innocent parties. The innocence of the teachers is primary in creating the drama's impact. A more timely and complex approach would have been a defense of the two women as

acknowledged lesbians. Although Karen and Martha are portrayed with sympathy and admiration, Martha's guilt, self-loathing, and ultimate suicide support the concept of perversion. Though she sustains the assaults of community accusations, her own realization of latent feelings towards Karen prove more than she can accept.

In most respects MacLaine's portrayal coincides with conventional notions of what lesbians are like. Looking slightly "butch," her short hair, round face, squarish body contrast with Hepburn's delicate silhouette. Their clothes further accentuate the difference. Martha refers to herself as a "shirt and blouse character." Her serviceable clothes look masculine next to the feminine dresses worn by Hepburn. It is interesting, however, that Hepburn also reveals subtle hints of latent homosexuality. Not only does she procrastinate about

The Children's Hour—with James Garner.

The Children's Hour

marrying Joe, but her physical characteristics (small breasts and narrow hips) bespeak of an androgynous figure.

Martha demonstrates other traits that have come to typify female homosexual behavior on the screen. Mellen has remarked that, despite the attempt of lesbians in society to be accepted as healthy, normal people, "the treatment of lesbianism in the film, however, has been marked by the view that lesbians are most often predatory. They appear either compulsively sadistic or masochistic, always possessive, jealous, hateful, and indeed sick."[6]

Martha's sharpness with Joe, lack of male companionship, outburst when Karen announces her marriage plans, and Aunt Lily's reference to her "insane devotion" reinforce the notion of Martha's jealousy and perversion. Martha herself believes this when she cries that she feels "sick and dirty."

In other ways the film is more sympathetic and less stereotypical than later movies. Mellen has complained that not one of the films about lesbians "recognizes that her homosexuality may not be the organizing principle of her life, that she may manifest outstanding achievement in non-sexual areas of her life."[7]

In large measure Martha functions as a competent individual who is leading a constructive life motivated by other than sexual concerns. Neither her work nor her relationship with the students is affected by her latent feelings, although homosexual boarding-school teachers have become a cliché. Further, the film emphasizes the warm feelings that can exist between two women whether or not there are sexual overtones. Certainly Martha's desire to spend their first money on clothes for Karen is a generous as well as a homosexual trait. Lastly, *The Children's Hour* stands foremost as a work that does not exploit a sadomasochistic relationship. Although Karen is considerably more stable and self-confident than Martha, neither woman dominates the other.

In preparation for *The Children's Hour*, MacLaine researched the question of latent homosexuality in women with several doctors. On the set, however, she was anything but serious. Wyler has commented that "Audrey, like most actresses, will require a moment to get herself in a proper mood for the scene, but Shirley—she will make jokes and clown it up until the last second. And then when the camera starts, she will be right in it. It's often disconcerting for the other people around."[8]

Besides the horseplay, MacLaine gave Wyler what he wanted. An associate claimed that Wyler was constantly fascinated by MacLaine's enormous range. "He keeps shooting take after take just to see what she'll come up with next time around."[9] Although it was not her first dramatic role, it was perhaps the most serious and complex to date. MacLaine explained, "Now you never know if Martha . . . is really guilty or whether she's driven to think she's guilty. That's what I had to do in acting it; it's very difficult, too, I might add."[10] Having worked with several top directors, MacLaine was well aware of what it meant to work with a pro. Referring to Wyler, Wilder, and others she told a film interviewer, "If . . . some of those people . . . wanted to film the telephone directory, I'd be apt to say yes. Because it's what's in their minds that's important, not so much what's in the script."[11]

Once again MacLaine appeared in a film that helped to redefine notions of sexuality on the screen and off. Following many months of pressure from the producers, *The Children's Hour* opened in January 1962 with a Production Code seal.

106

18

Two For the Seesaw

As Gittel in Robert Wise's version of *Two For the Seesaw* (1962), MacLaine plays another in the series of hard-luck kids. Gittel has been knocked around like Ginny in *Some Came Running* and Fran in *The Apartment,* yet she has emerged from these experiences with a sense of compassion for others. For this reason Marjorie Rosen can state that on the screen MacLaine made "kookiness sad, not elegant; promiscuity human, not trashy."[1] Although she is neither a feminist ideal nor a girl suitable "to take home to mother," Rosen asserts that MacLaine films helped to clear the air and loosen public inhibitions.

Two For the Seesaw is based on the 1958 Broadway success written by William Gibson, which starred Anne Bancroft and Henry Fonda. It deals with the complex, emotional relationship between two unlikely lovers—Gittel Mosca, a Jewish beatnik who lives in Greenwich Village, and Jerry Ryan (Robert Mitchum), a Midwest lawyer who comes to New York to start a new life while awaiting his divorce decree.

To prepare for the role, MacLaine spent time in the Village "getting to know the life of a broken-down Jewish dancer who thinks of herself as a doormat." According to MacLaine, "The Gittel I found wasn't William Gibson's Gittel, but she was enough like her and she was honest with me."[2] However, in reviewing the film, most critics took

exception to her interpretation, finding her Bronx accent and mannerisms blatantly false or criticizing the lack of a fully developed ethnic type. Clearly, the New York critics who reviewed the film would be expected to favor a localized characterization whose flavor was familiar and, therefore, so appealing. However, MacLaine's interpretation was consciously more universal. By playing down the specific traits of her urban, Jewish heroine, she was able to make the role of Gittel more meaningful to the general audiences across America who would see the film. It was not until the late sixties that the idiosyncratic mannerisms of New York Jews found expression in films like *Bye, Bye Braverman* (1968), *I Love You, Alice B. Toklas* (1968), and *Portnoy's Complaint* (1972). MacLaine's Gittel is slightly denatured, like Frank Sinatra as the Jewish son in *Come Blow Your Horn* (1963).

The difference in character is also the difference between Anne Bancroft and Shirley MacLaine. Whereas Bancroft's tough self-sufficiency seems to mask a neurotic core that runs very deep, MacLaine's nutty surface appears only as a cover for a basically healthy ego with little to hide. As played by MacLaine, Gittel's neuroses seem more like charming antics than psychological disturbances. Comparing the two actresses, Hollis Alpert stated that MacLaine's Gittel is "softer, cuter, and a little dopier." Certainly this lack of intelligence

Two For the Seesaw—with Robert Mitchum.

has marked many of MacLaine's portrayals, always tempered by a strong strain of natural common sense, which helps her grasp the reality of any situation.

In adapting the two-character play for the screen, Wise chose to open it up by adding exterior locations and several minor characters. He did, however, retain the concept of a double set by using a split screen for telephone calls between Gittel and Jerry—a gimmick that Andrew Sarris felt defeated Wise's efforts to create a mood of loneliness and isolation. The opening scene in a noisy Village apartment establishes the character of Gittel as a twenty-nine-year-old divorcée in ill-fitting clothes, who talks with food in her mouth, emotes with her hands, and peppers her conversation with the latest slang. In contrast, Jerry is ill at ease and down-in-the-mouth.

As the two develop an intimate relationship, it becomes clear that each possesses a slight touch of masochism. Jerry tells her she is a "born victim," yet at the same time he is himself anxious to be used. Intuitively Gittel understands this. In contrast to his indecisiveness and brooding moodiness, Gittel is cheerful and optimistic, letting her ulcers take the brunt of her problems.

As in other films, Gittel offers Jerry sexual compatibility because she genuinely likes him. Gittel does have her own notions of morality, though: she will never sleep with a man on the first date. Although defensive, Jerry cannot resist her niceness.

Each has a decided affect on the other. Gittel serves as a catalyst to help Jerry regain his sagging self-confidence, urging him to return to his profession. At the same time, Jerry tries to toughen up Gittel, pointing out how her move from job to job and from man to man is merely a defense against needing someone—a defense against commitment. But Jerry finds it hard to draw the line between encouragement and control. Like other MacLaine characters, Gittel submits to being made over by her lover. In a pathetic scene, she dances before a mirror in a Village loft that Jerry has helped her to find. Her seeming lack of talent is a tribute to MacLaine, whose true ability never shows through.

Eventually, Gittel decides to make a commitment and proposes marriage to Jerry. His inability to say, "I love you," convinces her that his heart never left Omaha despite the divorce decree. Gittel encourages him to return home, and the film ends with a telephone call—a final farewell. Despite the sad ending, we feel each has profited by the experience. Jerry will return to Nebraska more secure and mature than when he left. Gittel, having developed a better sense of self-worth, can now face the uncertain future with new strength.

Like *Lolita*, *The Chapman Report*, *The Children's Hour*, and the British film *A Taste of Honey* (all released in 1962), *Two For the Seesaw* deals with previously unexplored areas of sexuality from an adult point of view. Despite Hollywood's reluctance to fully explore the problems of fixation, frigidity, nymphomania, and lesbianism in these works, the films did initiate a move toward greater realism in film. Of all the above films, the sexual relationship portrayed in *Two For the Seesaw* is the most normal and, therefore, the most relevant. As shown in *Seesaw*, sex is a normal part of life, neither shameful nor sordid. Gittel is left alone at the end, not to pay for her crime of passion, but because she picked the wrong guy.

Two For the Seesaw

Two For the Seesaw

Perhaps next time she will be smarter.

Despite Gittel's sexual permissiveness, the film received no adverse publicity in this area. Rosen feels that the MacLaine persona, an "elfin, soulful innocence . . . shielded her from outrage," making her "avant-garde morality digestible."[3] To the extent that this was true, it reinforced the idea that sex was associated with girls who didn't know any better. The contradictions in Gittel's personality reflects the ambiguity of the times. It is easy to feel superior to a Gittel Mosca, but her warmth and genuine human needs make her universal.

In many ways *Seesaw* provides an unromantic look at the aging single female left to her own devices in the Big City—Fran Kubelik ten years hence or Meg Wheeler had she chosen adventure over marriage. The prospects are certainly bleak. Perhaps that is why Gittel, despite her inadequacies, deserves some credit for making it on her own.

Seesaw was released in August 1962. Most of the reviews were lukewarm, with general agreement as to the miscasting of both major roles. Most felt that it suffered by comparison with the play.

Two For the Seesaw

Two For the Seesaw

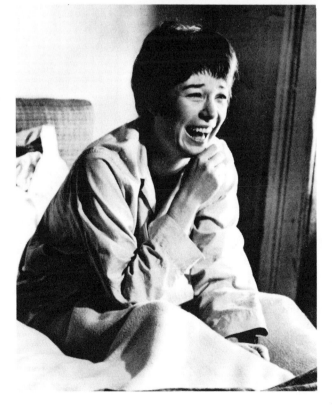

Two For the Seesaw

19

Irma la Douce

Although Elizabeth Taylor was Billy Wilder's original choice for *Irma la Douce,* Wilder had enjoyed the easy working relationship with MacLaine and Jack Lemmon in *The Apartment* and decided to recast them together in his new comedy based on the successful Broadway musical.

Like previous projects, the role of Irma provided MacLaine with an opportunity to discover more about people's lives and feelings. She plunged into her field research with great relish. Accompanied by a young Parisian friend, MacLaine visited a typical French hotel near Les Halles (the central market place of Paris—since demolished), which according to MacLaine is "one of the cheapest red-light districts in the world."[1] As described in her autobiography in amusing and sympathetic detail, her observations provided insight into the relationship between a *poule* (prostitute) and her *mec* (procurer), the women's sense of professional pride, and considerations regarding dress and body movements. All of this knowledge was incorporated into MacLaine's portrayal of Irma. She also learned of the oppression and subjugation of women, facts that never surface in Wilder's witty tale of life on the streets of Paris.

Irma la Douce depicted onscreen is the story of a successful, street-smart hooker and a good-natured, naive policeman named Nestor Patou (Jack Lemmon). As a new recruit, Nestor is appalled by the moral depravity he observes all around him. Despite bistro owner Moustache's (Lou Jacobi) worldy advice, he attempts to clean up the neighborhood by conducting an unauthorized raid, but only succeeds in losing his job. Later, unable to stand by while Hippolyte (Bruce Yarnell), Irma's *mec,* roughly mistreats her, Nestor comes to Irma's defense. With great effort he defeats Hippolyte and thus becomes Irma's new *mec.*

Nestor has been schooled on traditional notions of male-female relationships and wants Irma to stay at home while he goes out to earn a living. With wounded pride, Irma protests that it would be unthinkable for her *mec* to work. Jealous of Irma's innumerable clients, Nestor disguises himself as a wealthy, but impotent, Englishman, Lord X, and employs Irma to spend one evening each week with him in lieu of her other customers. For this he pays her a large sum of money.

Nestor is forced to take a job to secure sufficient funds to pay for Lord X's extravagance. Each evening after the two retire, Nestor sneaks out to nearby Les Halles where he works until dawn. Exhausted, Nestor is even too tired to make love, which convinces Irma that he is seeing another woman.

After a quarrel with Nestor, Irma succeeds in seducing Lord X. She is pleased with her ability to

Irma la Douce—with Jack Lemmon

restore his former virility. Nestor is less pleased, believing that Irma has fallen in love with his alter ego. Nestor takes Lord X's clothing down to The Seine, and fakes a drowning. Unfortunately Hippolyte discovers the floating clothes and reports his suspicions to the police. Nestor is arrested, convicted (without the *corpus delicti*) and sent to prison.

Months pass. One day Nestor hears of Irma's advanced pregnancy. With the help of Moustache and Irma's green stockings, he escapes from prison. To clear his name he arranges for Lord X's reemergence from The Seine and then rushes to the church to legitimize his coming child. The ceremony is barely complete when Irma goes into labor. Surrounded by her bridesmaids, all sisters of the night, Irma delivers a girl.

When *Irma la Douce* was released in June 1963 the reviews were mixed. Bosley Crowther obviously enjoyed "the antic romantic comedy," which he claimed was "an obvious needle of bourgeois morality,"[2] and *Time* called it "a raffishly sophisticated screen comedy."[3] However, Judith Crist, writing for *The New York Herald Tribune*, was bored by the "thrice-told and tritely told tale,"[4] and Hollis Alpert was put off by the beefed-up production. Few commented on the elaborate sets (the Mirisch brothers who produced the film imported great quantities of furnishing from Paris to create Rue Casanova) or cared much about the sixteen musical numbers deleted from the original stage version.

MacLaine's notices were universally glowing. Crowther liked her "wondrously casual and candid air that sweeps indignation before it and leaves one sweetly enamored of her."[5] Only Crist had reservations. Questioning her credibility, Crist felt MacLaine that resembled a "Sarah Lawrence girl on a sociological field trip in Pigalle."[6] The public had no such qualms. *Irma la Douce* was a huge

Irma la Douce—with Lou Jacobi.

success at the box office, earning $18,000,000 by 1965. Next to *Around the World in 80 Days* (which could not be called a MacLaine vehicle) it was MacLaine's biggest box-office success.

Like *The Apartment, Irma* is a satiric comedy that raises questions about conventional morality—specifically in the area of economics and sexuality. Like its predecessor, the plot revolves around the oppressors and the victims. However, in *Irma* the lines are not as clearly drawn. Further, by a clever role reversal, Nestor the *mec* becomes the victim, while Irma seems to command the scene.

In many respects the film is a moral story about immorality. Despite caustic comments about how prostitution helps the money circulation and the folly of being moral in an immoral world, the film closes on a rather conventional note—Nestor marries Irma and everyone lives happily ever after.

In an interview, Wilder referred to the story as "a nice clean, warm and sentimental story about the emancipation of a prostitute."[7] The picture doesn't quite support such a statement. *Irma* is clean and sentimental, alright. Wilder stayed well within the Production Code in depicting scenes of Irma on the job—and despite Irma's slit dress, dangling cigarette, green stockings, four-inch-high heels, and racy dialogue, the overall impression is one of innocence. Her rounded cheeks, pretty hair

Irma la Douce

bows, and white pet poodle capture the same childlike quality that made Ginny so incongruous in *Some Came Running*. In fact, MacLaine stated, "In this part, they couldn't have a girl who looks like a hooker who enjoys her work. That's why the standard Hollywood sex symbol in the role would be disastrous. This girl has to be a naïve, wide-eyed, innocent-looking young thing. Like I am."[8]

By emphasizing the wholesomeness of Irma, Wilder created another incarnation of the happy hooker—a male fantasy. By reinforcing this stereotype, the film implies that whores are really satisfied; that their life isn't so bad; and that if occasionally they are mistreated and knocked around, they can fend for themselves. (Here, Wilder must be credited with allowing the brutish violence that characterizes their way of life to peak through the general humor.) But most offensive is the implication that these women prefer prostitution. Opposed to reform, Irma's response to why she puts up with a *mec* is that "everybody needs somebody," a sad excuse for such ugly treatment.

Irma la Douce

115

Irma la Douce

Irma la Douce—clowning around on the set.

Obviously the events and dialogue are meant to be taken ironically. The real butt of the comedy is Nestor. In marvelous early episodes, Nestor parrots Victorian sentiments of morality, evidences shy embarrassment about sexuality, and stays at home while Irma works. Irma, on the other hand, has her own moral code, is wise in the ways of love-making, and produces the family income.

Liberation never occurs. The film opts for a sentimental fairy-tale ending. The problem is that in reversing the ironic twists, we see that once the roles are properly sought out, Irma can return to the home and take up where Nestor left off. Wilder's answer to prostitution then is legalized prostitution (marriage). However heartening Irma's cleverness and competence, the film implies that these are really male characteristics and thus comic when clothed in feminine apparel.

In the end, nothing changes on the Rue Casanova except that Nestor learns to mind his own business. The film surpresses the real endings, and MacLaine's only chance to reveal the truth came several years later in her own book.

Irma la Douce resulted in one of MacLaine's best performances. She was perfectly comfortable in a role that allowed her to exhibit her natural intelligence, self-confidence, and affability, and was funny without her usual quirky mannerisms and affected stupidity. For *Irma*, MacLaine received her third Academy Award nomination. Although the Oscar went to Patricia Neal for her role in *Hud*, MacLaine did win a Golden Globe, awarded by the Hollywood Foreign Press Association.

20

What a Way to Go!

Following the success of *Irma la Douce*, MacLaine signed to do a big-budget production with J. Lee Thompson, a British director-producer best known for *The Guns of Navarone*. *What a Way to Go* (1964) probably seemed like a sure winner on paper. The credits included a script by Betty Comden and Adolph Green (*Singin' in the Rain*), music by Jule Styne (*Funny Girl, Gypsy,* and *Three Coins in the Fountain*), choreography by Gene Kelly, costumes by Edith Head, photography by Academy Award winning cinematographer Leon Shamroy, and a cast starring MacLaine with six leading men—Dean Martin, Paul Newman, Robert Mitchum, Gene Kelly, Bob Cummings, and Dick Van Dyke. Filmed in CinemaScope and DeLuxe color, it looked as if the film couldn't miss. The missing ingredient, however, was the touch of a skilled director. The makings were all there, but Thompson was no master chef. He followed the basic recipe and concocted a present-able morsel, but somehow the whole thing never thoroughly jelled.

What a Way to Go! opens with an aerial view of Washington, D.C. Inside the Department of Inter-nal Revenue, Louise Benson (MacLaine), dressed in a simple black dress, attempts to give the United States government a check for $200,000,000. The scene then shifts to a psychiatrist's office where Mrs. Benson reveals to Dr. Stephanson (Bob Cummings) her guilt as one of the world's wealth-iest women.

Laid out on the couch, Mrs. Benson hysterically begins the tearful saga of her four tragic marriages, each of which left her richer than the one before.

Flashback! Louise tells of her childhood in a small American town. As Louise Foster, a simple country girl, she loves Edgar Hopper (Van Dyke), a poor, unambitious shopkeeper who spends hours drifting on the river, quoting Thoreau. Her social-climbing mother (Margaret Dumont) prefers young Leonard Crawley (Martin), the town's most eligible bachelor, but Louise is unimpressed with his money. She marries Edgar and all goes well until Crawley criticizes the manner in which Edgar supports her. Unwilling to allow the insult to go unchallenged, Edgar turns his attentions to busi-ness and builds Hopper's into the town's most prosperous store, which ruins Crawley. Edgar is overcome with hard work and dies suddenly, leaving Louise with $2,000,000.

Louise goes to Paris to forget her sorrow and meets a struggling young artist from Brooklyn, Larry Flint (Paul Newman). Attracted to his unspoiled nature, Louise marries Larry and takes up residence as a *bona fide* Bohemian. Their motto is "Money corrupts; art errupts." Larry listens to machine noises for inspiration. One day Louise feeds classical music into the machine and the

What a Way to Go!—with Gene Kelly.

machine paints a marvellous abstract painting. Realizing clients cannot distinguish a real painting from a manufactured one, Larry begins to merchandize these new works, thus becoming famous and wealthy. Larry becomes obsessed by his new invention and loses interest in his marriage. Finally, the machine goes berserk and strangles him to death. Once again Louise becomes a widow.

For a third husband Louise takes Rod Anderson (Robert Mitchum), a New York multimillionaire, hoping that his preexistent wealth will change her luck. Rod neglects his business to spend time with Louise, which only causes his stocks to triple. Louise believes she has once again cursed him with good fortune. She convinces Rod to retire and the two become gentlemen farmers. Louise feels triumphant, until Rod mistakenly tries to milk a bull and is kicked to death.

Louise's last husband is Jerry "Pinky" Benson (Kelly), an unsuccessful performer in a New York cafe. Like Louise, he wants a simple life. The two marry and live happily on a houseboat, until the night Louise suggests that Pinky do his act without his usual clown makeup. Heeding her advice, Pinky changes his act. Audiences respond enthusiastically, and overnight Pinky becomes a big star. Enamored with success, Pinky courts the crowds until one opening night when he is trampled by his adoring fans.

Louise finishes her tale of woe. As she leaves, she stumbles upon the janitor who turns out to be none other than Leonard Crawley, who has spent his recent years thinking of Louise and quoting Thoreau. Overcome with joy, Louise marries Leonard.

Back in Hopperville, Louise and Leonard live quietly with their four children. Suddenly an oil geyser gushes in their farmyard. Panicked, Louise concludes that the curse has returned, but it turns out that Leonard only punctured a company oil

What a Way to Go!—with Bob Cummings.

line. Louise hugs Leonard ecstatically as the camera cranes out.

The film was released in March 1964 and seemed to overwhelm most viewers. Critics complained of too many marriages, too many costumes, and too much MacLaine. *Time* summed it up as follows: "*What a Way to Go!* is five or six big, splashy movies rolled into none."[1] Everyone chose his own target. Stanley Kauffmann blamed the whole thing on Comden and Green, who he felt had "large comic ambitions and lesser comic abilities."[2] The British film journal, *Films and Filming,* felt that Thompson was responsible. And Judith Crist, not a member of the Shirley MacLaine fan club, felt drowned in the MacLainemania. However, despite such criticism, the film drew crowds and ended up number eight on the list of top grossers for 1964.

In terms of production, *What a Way to Go!* qualifies as an extravaganza *par excellence. My Fair Lady,* released the same year, cost $5,500,000. *What a Way to Go!* ran upwards to $5,000,000. Edith Head, working with a budget of $500,000, designed seventy-two costume changes for Mac-Laine, with a separate wig for each outfit. No doubt Miss Head, who had known MacLaine as far back as *The Trouble With Harry,* loved the chance to allow her imagination to run unfettered. In her book *The Dress Doctor,* Miss Head wrote, "Shirley fits into no mold or pigeonhole. She's the most completely uninhibited, completely honest person I've ever met."[3] Given seventy-two chances to capture MacLaine's personality, Head designed some of the wackiest, most outlandish costumes ever to hit the screen. Perhaps the *pièce de résistance* was the outfit Louise wears for Pinky's debut — a pink dress — with a pink wig and a pink Chinchilla coat.

In addition to stylish production numbers, *What*

What a Way to Go!

a Way to Go! contained another element that either delighted or annoyed critics: the film parodies. Today, when so many Hollywood products are remakes of earlier film classics *(The Black Bird, King Kong)*, a biography of a famous film star *(Gable and Lombard, W.C. Fields and Me)*, or a self-conscious film spoof of old movie conventions *(Blazing Saddles* and *Take The Money and Run)*, the brief episodes in *What a Way to Go!* hardly seem novel. But in 1964 such morsels were rather exceptional. As told by Louise, her first marriage was "like a wonderful old silent movie." What followed were comic bits, complete with slapstick routines recalling the Keystone Kops. A reminder of the zany sound comedies of yesteryear was the inclusion of Margaret Dumont (notable for her appearances with the Marx brothers), who played Mrs. Foster with great aplomb and exaggeration. Louise remembers marriage number two as being like "those wickedly romantic French movies." The love scenes that follow are straight out of

What a Way to Go!

What a Way to Go!

some subtitled film like Louis Malle's *The Lovers*. Louise characterizes the third marriage as looking like "one of those lush Hollywood movies" where upper-class characters march from one opulent set to another, wearing an endless array of high-fashioned clothing, in the Ross Hunter tradition. The last episode with Gene Kelly, probably the best of the series, is of course a spoof on Hollywood musicals, especially the Busby Berkeley variety. In fact, Pinky Benson's big premier is a parody of Comden and Green's own parody in *Singin' in the Rain*.

As for MacLaine in the role of Louise Foster-Hopper-Flint-Anderson-Benson-Crawley, although she takes on five married names, her personality remains basically the same. Underneath her sophisticated exterior beats the heart of a simple country lass. In essence, Louise spends the entire film trying to return to where she started. Each time she almost succeeds, but not quite. It is not until

What a Way to Go!—the heart of a simple country lass.

the finale that Louise, dressed in comfortable blue jeans, finally seems at home.

The message of this satire on the American success ethic is clear: "money is the root of all evil." Yet the moral never rings quite true, primarily because Louise seems so adaptable to the leisured life that only money can buy. Patricia Mills, writing for *Films in Review,* bemoaned this Cinderella story, crying, "If men don't put a stop to this nonsense the 'woman's picture' of a decade hence will *really* be something."[4]

Once again MacLaine plays an uneducated female who shines with practical wisdom. However, in the context of this film, such suggestions have disasterous results. Woman as inspirational muse is a fairly standard metaphor. In *What a Way to Go!,* the stereotype is comically distorted. As a benign, latter-day witch, Louise not only casts spells on others, but also works endless transformations on herself. Her ability to instill self-confidence in her erstwhile passive husbands is admirable. Unfortunately, these men seem incapable of controlling their own drives. It is too bad that in the end Louise is unable to find any creative outlet for herself other than that of a clotheshorse.

21

John Goldfarb, Please Come Home

After finishing *What a Way to Go,* MacLaine agreed to do another film with J. Lee Thompson—this time with Parker sharing the production credits. For screenwriter they hired a young friend, William Peter Blatty. Blatty was later to achieve fame as the author of the best-selling novel *The Exorcist,* and for the controversial film. With only two screen credits to his name, Blatty was still an unknown to most people.

Unfortunately, both Thompson and Blatty seemed off on their comic conceptions. They attempted to launch a satire, but they ended up with a travesty. For MacLaine, *John Goldfarb, Please Come Home* stands as the low-water mark in her otherwise shining career. Although she could blame *Artists and Models* (which has many saving graces) on Hal Wallis, the responsibility for *John Goldfarb* (which has almost no virtues) rests squarely on her own shoulders. Certainly with Parker as co-producer, she had as much control as actresses ever have. Perhaps the material looked better on paper, but even this is doubtful. Whatever, the film is no credit to anyone involved.

As Jenny Ericson, MacLaine plays a Pulitzer Prize winning reporter who is sent to Fawzia, disguised as a harem girl, to write a first-hand account of life inside a seraglio. Before leaving she has a brief but hostile encounter with John Goldfarb (Richard Crenna), former All-American halfback,

who is looking for the CIA offices. Unknown to Goldfarb, CIA Chief Heinous Overreach (Fred Clark) plans to send him on a U-2 mission over the Soviet Union. His candidacy is opposed, however, by others who consider his reputation a sizeable risk. Known in the press as Wrong-Way Goldfarb (a name coined by Ericson herself), Goldfarb has difficulty with directions and once ran a touchdown to the wrong goalpost.

Jenny arrives in Fawzia, where she quickly attracts the eye of King Fawz (Peter Ustinov), a lecherous old man who secretly spies on the harem bath, rides around his palace in a gold cart, and plays with toy trains. His one disappointment in life centers on the failure of his son, Prince Ammud (Patrick Adiarte), to make the football team of Notre Dame. In a fit of anger, Fawz breaks off relations with the United States and builds a football field of his own in the desert.

The unexpected arrival of Goldfarb (who has lost his way in the clouds and has crash-landed in Fawzia) raises the king out of the doldrums. Impressing Goldfarb into service as a football coach, Fawz prepares to challenge Notre Dame. Meanwhile, as Goldfarb attempts to transform a group of whirling dervishes into a forceful football team, Jenny cleverly finds ways to elude Fawz. She succeeds in convincing Goldfarb to choose her as his bed partner (courtesy of the king). But once

John Goldfarb, Please Come Home

out of sight of ole Fawz's eagle eye, their sleeping arrangements remain very separate.

The big event finally arrives. The all-star Notre Dame team arrives with instructions to save United States foreign policy by throwing the game. Following an orgiastic banquet aimed at reducing American efficiency, the two teams take to the field. Jenny leads the harem girls in a round of cheers and the game begins. At first Notre Dame has little trouble scoring against Fawzia U. But in the end, with the aid of questionable plays, oil geysers, and Jenny, the team pushes on to victory. Events are properly untangled and all ends happily. Unfortunately, the responses of the critics were not as happy.

The film was originally scheduled to open on Christmas Day 1964, but a suit filed and lost in New York State by The University of Notre Dame postponed the release until March 1965. Notre Dame claimed "the school's name and prestige had been misappropriated for commercial purposes without its consent," which damaged the university's reputation. The producers won their case but achieved only a Pyrrhic victory. The reviewers delivered their own verdict. Crowther wrote in *The New York Times:* "For this hodgepodge of political satire, horseplay and hoochy-koochy girls not only makes Notre Dame look foolish in a familiar low-comedy way, but it also demeans the prestige of movie humor and, indeed, of the human race."[1] No one had anything better to say.

Although Blatty may have had serious notions (he told a *Sports Illustrated* reporter that his inspiration came from the Francis Gary Powers's incident), the interviewer watching the chaotic location shooting in the Mojave Desert concluded that the film would "prove nothing more realistic than the fact that Shirley MacLaine . . . is as cute in football headgear and shoulder pads as she is in a harem costume and in any case, that she is a

125

John Goldfarb, Please Come Home

John Goldfarb, Please Come Home—in the harem.

John Goldfarb, Please Come Home—low burlesque.

loon."[2] Whatever Blatty's original conception, the result was a poor imitation of Stanley Kubrick's *Dr. Strangelove or: How I Learned to Stop Worrying and Love the Bomb*, released the previous year, which remains the classic satire on the foibles of international politics.

Even the final football game was a disappointment. It failed to accomplish what *M.A.S.H.* was later to do so well, and the gags and mishaps simply fell flat. Perhaps the director's unfamiliarity with the game was to blame. Audiences came away as confused as Thompson, who claimed, "Look here. The only real difference between the American game and ours is that you pass the ball forward and we pass it backward. And in that respect our game is much more artistic."[3]

MacLaine's initial appearance as a crackerjack reporter for *Strife* magazine gave hints of a tough-minded comic performance—perhaps like Rosalind Russell in Howard Hawks's *My Girl Friday*. At first, Jenny opposes the assignment, classifying the harem as a "vulgar, odious and

127

John Goldfarb, Please Come Home

repulsive" institution. Wearing a white suit and tie, and black-rimmed glasses, she is a logical setup for her boss, who accuses her of not being a woman. She is provoked into defending herself and takes the job.

Once in Fawzia, whatever intelligence and commitment she once possessed fades immediately. She dissolves into a dumb, screaming broad whose zany tricks are all aimed at protecting her virginity. Her slapstick stint (complete with blackened teeth and fright wig) sinks into low burlesque.

Comfortably installed in the female quarters of the palace, Jenny bathes in mountains of bubbles, learns to belly dance, and answers to "Number 28." The use of women as sexual objects to be parceled out as the men see fit brings no cries of rancor from the supposedly liberated Miss Ericson. (In fact, halfway through the film the whole notion of covering a story is somehow neatly dropped.) If the yellow sunsuit in *Artists and Models* offended MacLaine's sensibility, certainly the brief harem costumes and veils should have been equally odious.

John Goldfarb seems highly retrogressive for 1965, more sexist than any film MacLaine worked on. While offscreen she ventured into the remote Himalayan kingdom of Bhutan, onscreen she went from the frigid Miss Ericson to another version of the childlike prostitute with a heart of gold.

22

The Yellow Rolls-Royce

After the poor reception to the big-budget comedies *What a Way to Go* and *John Goldfarb, Please Come Home,* MacLaine flew to Europe to film one episode in Anthony Asquith's *The Yellow Rolls-Royce,* the last picture before his death in 1968. Asquith, who had directed British films since 1928, was respected as a competent though uninnovative artist. *The Yellow Rolls-Royce* (1965) was MacLaine's third production abroad (including *Around the World in 80 Days* and *My Geisha.*) and led to her long association with British film production. MacLaine had made twenty-one films since 1955, but she had been off the Hollywood set only five times (*The Trouble With Harry* and *Some Came Running* were both on location).

The Yellow Rolls-Royce, an original screenplay authored by the distinguished English playwright Terrence Rattigan (*The Winslow Boy* and *Separate Tables,* both later filmed), consists of three stories linked together by the presence of a yellow Rolls-Royce. The episode film that found great popularity in the midsixties, especially in Italy and France, came in several varieties. One version, usually a trilogy, starred two actors playing different roles under the hand of one director. Vittorio de Sica's *Yesterday, Today, and Tomorrow* (1964) with Sophia Loren and Marcello Mastroianni became the prototype, although antecedents go back much further. Other films utilized the talents of several directors and a whole array of stars *(Boccaccio '70* and *Rogopag—*both released in 1962). No doubt producers believed that a long list of notables could seduce dwindling audiences back into the movie theaters.

The emphasis on illicit love in *The Yellow Rolls-Royce* recalls one of the greatest episode films, Max Ophuls *La Ronde* (1950), remade in 1963. The opening episode of *The Yellow Rolls-Royce* occurs during the first quarter of the twentieth century and focuses on life among the titled rich. Its protagonist, the Marquess of Frinton (Rex Harrison), purchases the automobile as a surprise for his adored wife. Unfortunately, it is his surprise when he discovers Lady Frinton (Jeanne Moreau) and his assistant John Fane (Edmund Purdom) in the back seat of the custom-built limousine.

The theme of the first story reoccurs throughout the rest of the trio, with slight variations. Set in Italy in the 1930s, part two features a Miami gangster, Paolo Maltese (George C. Scott, in a wonderful and rare comic appearance) and his good-natured but trashy trollop, Mae Jenkins (MacLaine). Mae appears with short blond hair, painted fingernails, and layers of makeup, wearing a tight pink dress with black feathers and carrying an oversized patent-leather purse. When she opens her mouth, her flat voice and Brooklynese accent

The Yellow Rolls-Royce—with Art Carney and George C. Scott (with "violin" case).

confirm her lack of taste and education.

Paolo, who is tough but no more intelligent than Mae, is in Italy to soak up some culture. Mae has her own ideas about beauty and art. In Genoa, Paolo buys the yellow Rolls-Royce, which he refers to as the Royce-Rolls. Outgoing in her responses, Mae immediately falls in love with the car, which she fancies has a smile. Paolo and Mae set out for Pisa with fellow mobster Joey (Art Carney in his first screen appearance) as chauffeur. Although Paolo and Mae are engaged to be married, he often treats her brutishly, calling her "stupid" and "unfeeling" and slapping her on the ass. Mae accepts both his kindness and cruelty, often hiding her true emotions.

Unexpectedly, Paolo is recalled to the United States to finish off a rival. Left behind, MacLaine becomes sullen and bored and spends the day playing with her yo-yo. On a day's excursion to Sorrento, she meets a local photographer, Stephano (Alain Delon), whom she had previously spotted. The two find solace in one another's company.

Stephano takes Mae to the Blue Grotto. Here she reveals that she is a gangster's moll, but Stephano prefers to visualize her as a beautiful child who gives joy and happiness. He cautions her never to grow up. Mae tells Stephano that she loves Paolo and that he is the only person who has ever been good to her. But her true feelings belie her words. Later, Joey sees Stephano's shoes outside the Rolls-Royce.

When Paolo returns to Italy, Joey, with genuine concern, warns Mae to accept the facts of life and protect Stephano. Mae returns Stephano's photographs. She convinces him that Paolo's diamond bracelets and earrings mean more to her than the

The Yellow Rolls-Royce

psyche, Rattigan does afford us a glimpse of Mae from various perspectives. By placing Mae at the center of the narrative, he dignifies her and allows us to understand her situation and to identify with her feelings. In this respect her plight becomes a significant rather than a peripheral concern. Her objectification at the hands of Paolo thus seems even more tragic than Ginny's death, since we are cognizant of what Mae could become.

The role of Mae Jenkins did prove once again MacLaine's unique ability to play both comedy and pathos. As the brassy, gum-chewing strumpet whom Paolo brings to Italy, MacLaine showed off her mettle. In 1961 a *New York Herald Tribune* critic said,

> She (MacLaine) has a mastery of the sort of optimistic daze that has more than a blood relationship with the classic screen comedians of yesterday .... She can fling herself into slapstick without losing one whit of her characterizations, can live in a perpetual draft of confusion without losing her balance.[2]

The Yellow Rolls-Royce acknowledges this relationship when Mae, standing in front of a movie

love he can offer. Brushing aside her tears, she returns to Paolo (who has watched the whole scene behind a bush) and urges him to set a wedding date.

The last episode stars Ingrid Bergman as Mrs. Gerda Millett, a wealthy, older American woman, and Omar Sharif as Davich, a political refugee. Set in Trieste in 1941, the plot couples romance with political intrigue, with the Rolls serving the same function as in the preceding tales.

The film was released in February 1965. Critics were not terribly enthusiastic, although no one failed to note the polished look typical of all MGM products.

The role opened no new avenues for MacLaine but was a retreat to safe ground. As she had remarked concerning her image, "I had cornered the screen market on loose women."[1] As Mae, MacLaine plays a garden variety Hollywood whore—a hooker with a heart of gold and the intelligence of a twelve-year-old child. Both of these aspects were initially combined in the role of Ginny. But *The Yellow Rolls-Royce* contains one significant difference. Whereas we are never allowed to penetrate very deeply into Ginny's

The Yellow Rolls-Royce

The Yellow Rolls-Royce

132

poster, compares herself with the number-one platinum blond of the era—Jean Harlow. Like Harlow, MacLaine had comic timing and a marshmallow interior.

More touching, however, is the scene in which Mae feigns apathy towards Stephano to save his feelings and protect his life. Camille-like, she pretends to have a harlot's heart. Here, as the innocent waif, she generates true sympathy. Playing out an age-old female convention, she sacrifices true happiness to save her lover.

23

Gambit

After taking one step backward to play the role of a golden-hearted whore in *The Yellow Rolls-Royce,* MacLaine took another step back into familiar waters with *Gambit* (1966). Appearing once again as a spontaneous, loquacious bundle of energy, MacLaine played opposite Michael Caine in a *Topkapi*-like caper filled with wiley moves as complicated as any chess game.

The film opens with a detailed dramatization of the perfect heist. Only subsequently do we learn that the scene is only a fantasy of Cockney-born double-dealer Harry Dean (Caine). In a seedy Hong Kong nightclub, Dean and his assistant, French sculptor Emil Fournier (John Abbott), hire a Eurasian dancer, Nicole Chang (MacLaine) to assist them in a plan to steal a priceless Chinese statue. With the promise of $5,000 and a British passport, Nicole agrees to pose as Harry's wife but is not told of their criminal intent.

Immediately Harry and Nicole fly to meet Moslem multimillionaire, Ahmad Shahbandar (Herbert Lom), whose late, beloved wife closely resembled Nicole. After giving the slip to hired heavies, the two make contact with Shahbandar and lunch with him on his personal yacht. Nicole charms him, and the couple is invited to see his private apartments. Once there, Shahbandar, suspicious of the couple, gives Harry and Nicole an impressive demonstration of the electronic security

devices he maintains to protect his prized sculpture of an Empress, which was brought from the Orient by Marco Polo. Astonishingly, Nicole bears a marked resemblence to the ancient queen.

Anxious to spend more time with Nicole, Shahbandar invites the two for dinner. Harry declines but accepts for Nicole. Nicole is pleased with her success and only now learns the real nature of Harry's plans. At first she refuses to go along with the scheme, but finally she allows her feelings for Harry to overcome her reservations.

That evening, while Shahbandar entertains Nicole in the Arab quarters, Harry sneaks into his apartments and attempts to steal the statue. Nicole leaves her host to warn Harry that Shahbandar is wise to his game. When Harry refuses to reconsider, Nicole agrees to stay and help. In a long, silent scene Nicole climbs through a dome and agilely lifts the statue off its pedestal. As the two are about to escape, Harry declares his love and Nicole, unable to restrain her joy, steps forward and sets off an alarm. Nicole escapes to the roof; Harry hides. In an unexpected move, an armed guard checks a hidden alcove, revealing the real statue.

However, when Shahbandar returns to his apartment, he is distressed to discover in a second reversal that the statue in the alcove is a fake. He apprehends Nicole inside the airport and warns her that unless the real statue is returned Harry's life

Gambit—with Michael Caine and John Abbott.

will be in danger. Nicole returns to Hong Kong to alert Harry. In a further twist, Harry claims he did not steal the statue but only hid it in Shahbandar's apartment. His plan is to generate publicity about the theft so that he can sell Emile's carefully fabricated copies to unsuspecting art dealers who believe they have a hot object.

Declaring swindle worse than theft, Nicole bows out. In yet another surprise, Harry reaffirms his love and smashes the Chinese head as an act of good faith. After the two lovers kiss and leave, Emile, in the film's final irony, opens a cupboard revealing three more fake statues ready for the black market. The gambit has worked.

The film was released in November 1966 to unanimous praise by delighted reviewers. Hollis Alpert had glowing comments for the film's novelty, performances, and Ronald Neame's direction. The *Time* reviewer compared the film favorably with *Topkapi,* especially MacLaine's long scene, which he termed a pretty "piece of acro-

batic larceny." *The New York Times,* happy with all the actors, claimed that "the writers, the director, and the tyro but talented producer manage to pull it all off while keeping tongues in cheeks."[1] *Variety* called the film "topnotch suspense comedy-romance, expert in all departments,"[2] and Judith Crist said, "*Gambit* is a delightful mixture of fun and larceny, bright and beguiling and boasting at least four of the neatest plot twists pulled on the screen."[3]

Most of all, Crist was pleased about MacLaine. Recovered from her adverse reactions to *Irma la Douce* and *What a Way to Go,* she noted: "Let me give you advance notice too of Shirley MacLaine who had been getting louder and louder and more and more frenetic by the film. This time out, courtesy, we suspect, of director Ronald Neame, Miss MacLaine is the Shirley we fell for 'way back,' a deft and subtle comedienne and a thoroughly charming and warmly appealing young woman."[4]

Miss Crist was correct that the MacLaine on the

135

Gambit—with Michael Caine.

screen harkened back to older images. Once again MacLaine played the slightly dopey girl of natural talents who eventually proves her worth. Like characters in *Ask Any Girl*, *My Geisha*, and *John Goldfarb, Please Come Home*, Nicole must don a disguise to accomplish this task. As in previous films, the elements of the disguise are carefully selected to please a male character and are thus seductive in nature. Left on her own, Nicole is innocent and inquisitive, with a scrubbed face. Coupled with Harry, she becomes a flashy, made-up, bejeweled, high-fashion doll. Again there is a split between the two personalities. The real Nicole is childlike and engaging. The false Nicole is proper and stoney-faced, like the stone object they plan to steal — an object of beauty for men's eyes.

The real Nicole is alive and human, according to Harry "too human." The false Nicole is dead like Shahbandar's wife and the inanimate statue.

Like the single women in MacLaine's films of the early sixties, Nicole is a self-possessed, hard-working female, alone in the world. For a moment we even believe that she has reformed her man, as was common in the earlier comedies, but the film's final twist proves otherwise. However, though Harry outsmarts Nicole, she gets him on her own terms. She returns to her former self, without the makeup and fancy clothes, and Harry takes her as she is. Together they form the ideal couple — a perfect blend of intuition and reason, spontaneity and premeditation.

Despite the critics' praise, *Gambit* was only a moderate success at the box office. Seen today, the film appears rather ordinary, the characterizations reactionary for 1966. But the elaborate heist scenes still manage to capture the imagination.

24

Woman Times Seven

Carrying forward the current fashion for episodic films like *What a Way to Go* and *The Yellow Rolls-Royce,* MacLaine agreed to star in the Joseph E. Levine production *Woman Times Seven* (1967). On paper the film looked auspicious. Vittorio de Sica, the great Italian director, was hired as director, for what was to be his only American film. Italy's foremost screenwriter and film theorist Cesare Zavattini, was hired to write an original script. Together, these two men had created film history, producing such neorealistic masterpieces as *Shoeshine* (1946), *The Bicycle Thief* (1948), *Miracle in Milan* (1950), and *Umberto D* (1952). Later, Zavattini became the driving force behind the pioneer modern episode film *Love in the City* (1953). Subsequently, the two men teamed up again on less serious, but more successful, sex comedies such as *Boccaccio '70* (1961) and *Yesterday, Today and Tomorrow* (1963).

The picture, filmed on location in Paris and at the Boulogne Studios, begins with the story of Paulette (MacLaine) called *Funeral Procession.* Dressed in black, face stained with tears, Paulette follows the coffin of her late husband. Tenderly, her companion Jean (Peter Sellers) attempts to comfort her. As Jean declares his love, Paulette's spirits slowly revive. The two make plans to go off together and become so engrossed in their conversation that they inadvertently miss a turn in the

road. Separated from the rest of the funeral procession, the new lovers never notice the reactions of the shocked mourners.

Story number two, *Amateur Night,* centers on an upper-middle class Italian housewife, Maria Teresa (MacLaine), who arrives home one night to find her husband Georgio (Rossano Brazzi) in bed with another woman. Determined to find revenge, she flees the apartment, vowing to bed the first man she finds. Maria Teresa is encouraged in this enterprise by a group of street walkers who arrange a meeting with one of their best clients. However, Maria Teresa is frightened when she discovers that the client in the car is stark naked. The girls are disappointed with Maria Teresa's equivocations and angered by her willingness to let her husband "get away with it," and they send her home with their procurer. In front of her apartment, the procurer socks Georgio for insulting Maria Teresa. Immediately Maria Teresa runs to her wayward husband and soothes his bruises.

The third episode, *Two Against One,* features MacLaine as an international interpreter named Linda. Vivacious and attractive, Linda invites two representatives from the International Cybernetics Congress — a young Italian (Vittorio Gassman) and a Scotsman (Clinton Greyn) — back to her apartment for a poetry reading. Nude under a blanket, Linda regales them with stories of how her lover

Woman Times Seven—MacLaine as Eve.

Bob admires her for spiritual and intellectual qualities. When one man touches her, she quickly angers. Both men confess their desires and then proceed to slap one another in a display of contriteness. Sexually stimulated by this show of penitence, Linda throws out Bob's photograph and jumps into bed.

Set in England, episode number four, *The Super-Simone*, deals with a popular novelist (Lex Barker) and his plain, unassuming wife, Edith (MacLaine). Husband Vic has created a big success with his fictional femme fatale, Simone. Simone is cynical, moody, and changeable, and appears to Edith as the perfect woman. After long hours of fantasizing about this exciting incarnation of womanhood, Edith decides to alter her appearance in hopes of becoming exciting like Simone. Dressed à la Baby Snooks, she slides around the apartment on roller skates. Vic, who genuinely loves the once quiet Edith, decides that she is crazy and calls in a

Woman Times Seven—MacLaine as Maria Teresa.

138

Woman Times Seven—MacLaine as Linda, with Vittorio Gassman and Clinton Greyn.

psychiatrist (Robert Morley) to diagnose the problem. Too late, Edith realizes her mistake and runs onto the rooftop screaming, "I'm done in."

Back in France, Eve, the upper-class heroine of the fifth story, *At the Opera,* prepares for the evening opera. Outraged by her discovery that another woman plans to wear an identical gown to the grand event, she calls upon her husband (Patrick Wymark) to be a man and sets about sabotaging her friend's efforts. An employee is dispatched to bomb the rival's limousine and Eve arrives at the Opera House in elegant splendor. To her dismay, she spies a short, dumpy woman in the same dress. Humiliated, she leaves the theater. On her way down the grand staircase, she encounters her rival, besmirched from the auto explosion but intent upon making a grand entrance. Anticipating the rivals shocked reaction to the third woman, Eve sits down and uncontrollably breaks into laughter.

The sixth tale, *The Suicides,* concerns the plight of two lovers, Marie (MacLaine) and Fred (Alan

Woman Times Seven—MacLaine as Linda.

Woman Times Seven—MacLaine as Edith.

Woman Times Seven—MacLaine as Eve.

Woman Times Seven—MacLaine as Marie, with Alan Arkin.

Arkin) who conclude a suicide pact. Gravely serious and overtly nervous, the two are sequestered on the top floor of a seedy hotel. They bemoan Fred's marriage to an older woman and record their final words into a tape recorder, declaring their sanity and desire to perform this act of independence against a hostile world. Marie wants to die in her wedding dress. Fred is against pills and plans to use a gun. After making love for the last time, Marie goes into the bathroom. Alone, Fred rethinks his decision and sneaks out of the room. On his way out he sees Marie, already halfway down the fire escape. The two bid one another a fond farewell.

The last story, *Snow*, stars MacLaine as a shy, upper-middle-class housewife, Jeanne. As Jeanne shops with her beautiful friend (Anita Ekberg), she notices that they are being followed by a handsome, young stranger (Michael Caine). At home with her husband (Phillippe Noiret), Jeanne is flattered to see the man standing below her window in the snow. She fantasizes dreamily about the mysterious stranger, never realizing that he has been hired by her jealous husband to follow her.

The critics were unimpressed with the efforts of MacLaine, de Sica, and Zavattini. Following the film's release in June 1967, each suffered his own attack. Implying that more often equals less, the *Time* reviewer compared MacLaine's seven impersonations unfavorably against Sophia Loren's three in *Yesterday, Today, and Tomorrow*. He blamed Zavattini's "amateurish anecdotes" and claimed that de Sica should have known that "a tour de force is like a striptease; there is no point in the performance if the material does not come off in style."[1]

Time also complained that MacLaine seldom deviated from "her customary screen self," and all of the critics questioned the degree to which the seven stories actually probed into the various facets

Woman Times Seven—MacLaine as Jeanne.

of womanhood. However, Bosley Crowther was most perceptive in articulating the problem. Noting the basic misogyny, Crowther commented:

> For a man who has treated women as nicely as Vittorio De Sica . . . it is shocking and thoroughly bewildering to find him kicking them around as he does in his new picture, *Woman Times Seven*. Not one of the seven silly females whom Shirley MacLaine portrays in this series of seven blackout sketches provokes any feeling but disgust — or possibly embarrassment and pity — for the weaker (shall we say minded?) sex. Not one of them has the charm, the humor or the vitality we've come to expect in Mr. De Sica's women.[2]

In an attempt to explain the cause of such a turnabout, he continues,

> All one can reasonably imagine is that Mr. De Sica and Cesare Zavattini wrote the script, got so completely snarled in the English language and in the American zaniness of Miss MacLaine that they lost their own Latin sense of humor and had nothing to put in its place.[3]

Only *Variety* reviewer Murf seemed generally pleased with the whole affair.

On the surface the film seems to represent a cross-section of women. Paulette, Eve, and Jeanne are French; Maria Teresa and Marie, Italian; and Linda and Edith, English. Eve is upper class; Paulette, Maria Teresa, and Jeanne, upper-middle class; Linda and Edith, middle class; and Marie and the prostitutes, lower class. Eve is glamorous; Edith, plain. Linda is unattached and sexually free; Maria Teresa, married and inhibited. Paulette is a pragmatist; Jeanne, a dreamer. Eve is a self-centered, egotistical bitch; Edith thinks only of pleasing her husband.

However, like the women in *What a Way to Go*, the heroines of *Woman Times Seven* are only superficially differentiated. Each appears as a mere caricature, defined by one overriding lack. Granted, the male characters fare little better, but given the premise of the film, we are led to expect

142

more insight into the woman's world. Paulette is a hypocrite who lacks steadfastness. Maria Teresa, though wronged, lacks the ability to assert herself. Linda, a pseudointellect and sexual tease, lacks insight into her own motivations. Edith, a pathetic soul, lacks maturity and a positive self-image. Eve, perhaps the most vile of all, is trivial and destructive and lacks any trace of basic humanity. Marie, in what is probably the most engaging of the seven stories, lacks levity but eventually does face up to the truth of the situation. Lastly, Jeanne, though gentle and demure, lacks personality and assertiveness. Practically all of the women are moody and changeable, reinforcing the stereotype of woman as an unreliable, emotional being. All either rely on men for emotional sustenance or a sense of self-worth, or brutally use men for their own purposes. None of the women display individual ambitions or personal commitments. Not surprisingly, none of the stories depict a mutually satisfying relationship between the sexes. Most glaring, however, is the immaturity of the seven women and their total lack of self-perception.

Perhaps the stories could be interpreted as a portrayal of the plight of women in the modern world. Unfortunately, such a reading is made suspect by the cruel, ironic treatment by both de Sica and Zavattini of all but the lower classes. Only the prostitutes of *Amateur Night* and Marie of *The Suicides* elicit any sympathy. One of the most revealing moments occurs when one whore asks, "Got man troubles?" The immediate bond forged between women of different worlds is the highlight of the film. But as the prostitutes discover, the revolution will be slow in coming.

Almost every episode ends with the sellout of a woman — usually to a man. The ironic truths that end each section ultimately work to expose the women as petty, silly, or self-deluded. Upper-class women are spoiled and mean; middle-class women, weak and insecure.

In 1952, still inspired by a cinema of naturalism and truth, Zavattini wrote, "My fixed idea is to deromanticize the cinema; I want to teach people to see daily life with the same passion they experience in reading a book."[4] The gap between these ideals and the myths of *Woman Times Seven* are shattering. In place of living characters, Zavattini created caricatures, and in place of complications, he produced clichés. It is regrettable that he did not turn his pen to a more serious task, for surely he might have provided some fresh answers to the age-old question "What is a woman?"

25

Sweet Charity

The poor reception of *Woman Times Seven* added one more film to a growing list of disappointments. Going from one extravaganza to another, MacLaine seemed to be thrashing around in search of the right part. Not since Irma was there an interesting, dynamic character who could challenge her creativity and capture the public imagination. The multiple roles in *What a Way to Go* and *Woman Times Seven* may have offered variety, but they were no substitute for one viable personality.

MacLaine's films had become more and more obvious — parodies of earlier works. They relied on old clichés, familiar character types and big budgets, and lavish productions to compensate for weak scripts and second-rate directors. Left to her own devices by undemanding directors, her mannerisms became more and more frantic; frenzy replaced subtlety.

Therefore, when the opportunity arose to bring to life the heroine of Universal's new film production of *Sweet Charity*, MacLaine jumped at the chance to bolster her sagging career. The role was ideal for MacLaine. For years she had built a career playing kooks, waifs, and prostitutes. Charity combined all three characteristics in one role. The part seemed written for her — the culmination of her years in Hollywood.

But Universal was taking no chances. Despite MacLaine's star status, her recent ratings at the box office were less than spectacular. Hedging their bet, Universal budgeted $10,000,000 to launch what they hoped would be the musical motion picture of the seventies, on the theory that the way to make money was to spend it. Having signed MacLaine, the foremost "Hollywood hooker" of the era, the producers decided to gamble on novice director Bob Fosse, who had directed and choreographed the original 1966 Broadway production starring his wife, Gwen Verdon. Charity was the second film role Verdon lost to MacLaine. In 1960, 20th Century passed over Verdon in favor of MacLaine when they cast *Can-Can*.

Sweet Charity opens with the announcement that the film is the "adventures of a girl who wanted to be loved." We are immediately introduced to Charity (MacLaine), a tall, fleshy redhead who sports a tatoo on her left shoulder, which reads "Charlie." After expressing her joys about New York City in "My Personal Property," Charity is suddenly pushed off a Central Park bridge into the water below by Charlie, who then runs off with her life savings.

Refusing to be disheartened despite a heavy heart, Charity defends Charlie to her friends and co-workers (Chita Rivera and Paula Kelly) at the Fandango Ballroom, where she works as a taxi dancer and "social consultant." Her friends accuse her of having a "heart like a hotel." Together, the

Sweet Charity

girls, lined up behind a railing, perform the provocative production number "Hey Big Spender," intended to entice customers, but which also reveals their hostility. Charity, unable to hold back her tears, cries and admits she's a pushover.

Out on the street, Charity accidentally stumbles upon Italian movie idol Vittorio Vitale (Ricardo Montalban) in the midst of a quarrel with his superstar Ursula. Unexpectedly Vittorio invites Charity to the exclusive Pompeii Club, where dancers perform the sophisticated "Rich Man's Frug." Later at Vittorio's apartment, she dines elegantly and sings, "If My Friends Could See Me Now." Unfortunately, the reappearance of Ursula necessitates that Charity spend the rest of the evening in a closet.

Charity decides to improve her life and goes to an employment service, but discovers that she is unqualified for any respectable position. As she leaves the building, Charity finds herself stuck in an elevator with Oscar Lindquist (John McMartin), a conservative, young insurance man who suffers from claustrophobia. She endears herself to Oscar by keeping a cool head, and he asks to see her again. He is taken by her warmth and gentleness and names her Sweet Charity.

Two weeks later the two attend a hip revival meeting conducted by Big Daddy (Sammy Davis, Jr.), who preaches the "Rhythm of Life." When the police raid the services, Charity and Oscar hide in a stack of tires. Having miraculously lost his claustrophobia, Oscar attributes his good fortune to Charity and proposes marriage.

Charity, happy at last, quits her job, tells Oscar the truth about herself, and exuberantly leads a parade, singing, "I'm a Brass Band." However, at the marriage bureau, Oscar has his first chance to meet Charity's friends and to notice her tatoo. Shamefacedly, Oscar admits that the other men in Charity's life do bother him and, asking her forgiveness, bows out. Charity begs, but Oscar claims he cannot change his attitudes.

Charity is abandoned once again and returns to the bridge in Central Park where Charlie had once deserted her. She sits there all night. In the morning, a group of flower children give her a daisy. Reacting to this gesture of love, Charity smiles and slowly goes off into the distance. The closing title appears, "And she lived hopefully ever after."

Sweet Charity was released in February 1969. It did not prove to be the "big picture" that Universal was hoping for, but it did arouse much controversy. Critical fever ran high and everyone had their say. For the most part, reviewers were either for or against. Some, like Joseph Gelmis of *Newsday*, called *Sweet Charity* "a superb movie musical." More unrestrained, *Variety* claimed that the film would "become one of the memorable artistic and commercial successes of this genera-tion."[1] On the other end of the spectrum, Vincent Canby saw the film as "enlarged and so inflated that it has become another maximal movie; a long, noisy and, finally, dim imitation of its source material."[2]

Most of the critics agreed that the film (and for that matter the stage show as well) was a pale reworking of Federico Fellini's *The Nights of Cabiria* (1957), on which both musicals were based. Reviewers were quick to point out that MacLaine lacked the poignancy of Giulietta Masina, whose large eyes and innocent face made Cabiria a memorable character. Only Andrew Sarris

145

Sweet Charity—with director Bob Fosse.

Sweet Charity—with Ricardo Montalban.

of *The Village Voice* took issue with such a simplistic approach, stating, "the biggest problem is that *Cabiria* takes place, however fantastically, in Italy whereas *Sweet Charity* takes place, however fancifully, in America, and the milieu is always at least part of the message."[3]

Summing up the argument most cogently, Arthur Knight, writing for *The Saturday Review*, offered perhaps the final word: "In short, if one had never heard of *Nights of Cabiria*, *Sweet Charity* might appear a superior musical with a somewhat inferior book; whereas the truth, if anyone connected with this production had sought to attain it, is just the other way around."[4]

Opinions of Fosse's direction also varied. Clearly, Fosse was a new talent to be reckoned with. A proven creator of freshness and style (who had served as dance director on several films), his mannered, contorted choreography always bore a stamp that marked the dance as uniquely his own. No one questioned his obvious understanding of cinematic possibilities or failed to predict a bright

Sweet Charity—with John McMartin.

Sweet Charity—MacLaine dances to the music of "I'm a Brass Band."

future (later proved by his 1972 Academy Award as director of *Cabaret*). However, not all approved of his self-conscious camera effects and rhythmic editing techniques. According to MacLaine, Fosse was getting inside Charity with a camera. *Washington Post* critic Gary Arnold felt suffocated by Fosse's endless 70-mm closeups and was irritated by his manipulative editing.

As for MacLaine, Gelmis claimed that "Shirley MacLaine, as the naive waif, gives the best performance of her career."[5] Charles Champlin of *The Los Angeles Times* echoed these same sentiments, claiming that MacLaine "brings off superbly the rather peculiar challenge that a musical presents: to do a singing and dancing performance . . . yet also to create a character who has some validity . . . . (It) is Miss MacLaine's finest hour."[6] On the other hand, Sarris responded poorly to the nervous

hysteria of MacLaine's performance, and *Newsweek* writer Joseph Morgenstern felt that "MacLaine's sweet simplicity is so insistent that your heartstrings are less tugged at than clawed at."[7]

Fosse's own conclusions are interesting. Having worked with MacLaine as far back as *The Pajama Game*, which he choreographed on Broadway, he remembered her as "a pleasant girl with a kind of circus in her face."[8] In an interview comparing Gwen Verdon with MacLaine he stated that Verdon had a Chaplinesque fragility and that Shirley's Charity was more earthy. "Shirley has an intimate movie style which catches the essence of Charity, an ability to convey the girls inner pain and still keep the outward bubble going."[9]

MacLaine had a special affection for Charity and easily identified with her character. During filming she stated, "I gravitate to optimistic characters who don't hedge their bets — I'm like that myself.

Sweet Charity—the bridge in Central Park.

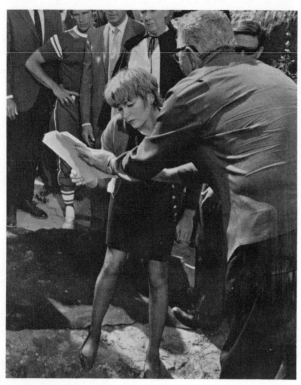

Sweet Charity

I believe you should just let it all hang out there, honestly and openly, that's what love and today are all about."[10]

Remembering the embarrassment of *Can-Can*, MacLaine began preparing for *Sweet Charity* two and a half months before the other dancers were even called in. Working with Gwen Verdon, she threw herself into a disciplined dance training. The dedication shows. Although MacLaine lacks the suppleness and skill of veteran Gwen Verdon, her dancing in *Sweet Charity* was certainly defensible.

26

The Bliss of Mrs. Blossom

MacLaine's next film, *The Bliss of Mrs. Blossom* (1968), offered a whole range of new possibilities. Still within the realm of film comedy, Mrs. Blossom allowed MacLaine an opportunity to play a mature, modern woman and to deal with topics such as infidelity and sexual fantasy. The fact that these issues are presented with tongue-in-cheek does not detract from their relevance.

Set in England, *The Bliss of Mrs. Blossom* chronicles the story of Robert (Richard Attenborough) and Harriet (MacLaine) Blossom, who have been married twelve years. He is a bullish, successful brassiere manufacturer who is always at the office; she is a bored housewife, originally from Columbus, Ohio, who spends the day working at her sewing machine. One day the machine breaks down and Robert sends repairman Ambrose Tuttle (James Booth) to the rescue. Ambrose, after a mean game of pool with Harriet, reveals that he is an orphan. Harriet, taking pity on his plight, offers him a bed in the attic. It is not long before they discover a special affinity. At the first kiss, sparks fly and stars appear.

That evening when Robert returns home, Harriet greets him cheerfully. While Robert devotes himself to his favorite pastime, music, Harriet dreamily thinks about Ambrose and smiles.

Two foppish detectives (Freddie Jones and William Rushton) appear the next day in search of the missing repairman, but can find no traces of Tuttle, who is now permanently installed in the attic. The three subsequently settle down to a ménage à trois (although Robert remains ignorant of the true events). At night Robert conducts the great symphonies of the world, all played on his home hi-fi. Harriet knits, reads, and later takes up painting. Up above, Tuttle listens to the music, redecorates his apartment, and takes up carpentry, physical fitness, and eventually financial investing.

During the day, after Robert leaves for work, Harriet and Ambrose live out their fantasies of famous love stories like *The Three Muskateers*, *Doctor Zhivago*, and *St. George and the Dragon*. Although Harriet has occasional moments of guilt, and even once decides to end her double life, she finally concludes that making two men happy (including herself) is a worthy endeavor. Filled with new confidence, she even embarks upon a successful painting career. Meanwhile, Robert, concerned about the noises he hears at night and objects that seem to be missing from his home, consults a psychiatrist (Harry Towb).

Things go from bad to worse, and Robert begins to question his sanity. Finally he suffers a complete mental breakdown. At this point, Ambrose, who has developed a special affection for Robert over the past three years, steps in and revitalizes Blossom Brassieres. Ambrose puts the company

The Bliss of Mrs. Blossom—with Richard Attenborough.

back on its feet, relying on his self-learned business acumen and tips that he feeds to Harriet. Robert recovers and Blossom Brassieres surges ahead to become a leader in the field. Robert even makes the cover of *Time*.

Secure at the top of his profession, Robert conceives of developing a universal brassiere, which he hopes to merchandise to the poor nations of the world. As he states, "The only underdeveloped man is woman." To unveil his new creation, Robert organizes a huge convention in Switzerland, where he plans to move (to a new home *sans* attic). Unable to live without Harriet, Ambrose sabotages the exposition. When the bra-clad models begin to inflate their brassieres, they discover to their dismay that they cannot control the air supply. In moments, hundreds of beauties are absurdly floating in the air. Everyone is embarrassed and Robert is practically ruined.

The detectives, still on the trail of the missing Tuttle, finally discover the truth. This leads to a quick divorce and Harriet then marries Ambrose. Robert, feeling no animosity towards the illicit couple, gives them his house and factory and decides to devote himself to music.

The film ends on a typical day. Ambrose rises early and rushes off to the office. As Harriet sits down with her trusty sewing machine, the floor opens, and rising from the cellar is Robert, her new lover.

Unfortunately, this delightfully wry, ironic film arrived and left before anyone could bat an eye, although some critics managed to catch it during its brief run. Andrew Sarris called it the sleeper of the year — "a bubbling, sparkling, civilized comedy of marital and extra-marital manners, an exercise in stylistic sublimation."[1] The film opened on 4 October 1968 during the barrage of holiday releases. The *New York Times* didn't even run a review until 12 December.

The Bliss of Mrs. Blossom—with James Booth.

The Bliss of Mrs. Blossom

Although the story of an adulterous relationship was hardly new fodder, *The Bliss of Mrs. Blossom* offered some novel twists. Sprinkled with witty dialogue and visual metaphors — all beautifully enhanced by the understated performances of the principles — the film emphasized joy, unorthodoxy, and the pleasure of a fully lived fantasy life. Only once is sin referred to. Harriet, aware of her ecstatic state, decides that her life must be wicked, but she immediately suppresses such a conventional notion.

No doubt *The Bliss of Mrs. Blossom* was conceived as little more than a clever bedroom farce; however, the film is filled with such vitality and human warmth that some word must be said of its difference from most marital comedies. Ultimately, goodwill takes precedence over sophistication. Perhaps because a woman stands at the center of the work, the lovers never appear to be

exploited nor decline into petty, jealous rivals. And unlike movies of the past where adulterous wives paid with their lives *(The Postman Only Rings Once* and *The Lady From Shanghai),* or are presented as evil *(The Graduate),* Harriet remains alive and charming.

Most important is the film's emphasis on fantasy. In one respect, the whole film is a romantic, female fantasy of one woman's ideal world. On another level, the individual fantasy sequences, complete with gorgeous costumes, handsome heroes, and exotic locations, typify the female sensibility. Male fantasies, on the other hand, tend to emphasize beautiful, busty women, passive female sex objects, or supportive housewives, nurses, and maids. Appropriately female, the dream sequences establish men as the source of pleasure for women — a nice reversal. In a unique way, *The Bliss of Mrs. Blossom* openly acknowledges women's sexual needs as being on a par with those of men.

As Harriet Blossom, MacLaine provided an ideal offbeat charm, blending a perfect mixture of innocent sensuality and nonchalant sophistication. Sarris commented that "Shirley MacLaine is the biggest revelation in the most restrained performance of her career."[2]

Although *The Bliss of Mrs. Blossom* was only MacLaine's second film made in England (*The Yellow Rolls-Royce* was first), it followed a long and happy association with British directors (J. Lee Thompson, Anthony Asquith, Ronald Neame, and now Joseph McGrath). The British journal *Films and Filming* may have voiced some reservations about *The Bliss of Mrs. Blossom,* but MacLaine's film had always done well in England and she was one of the most popular box-office attractions.

27

Two Mules for Sister Sara

MacLaine's impersonation of an adulterous house-wife in *The Bliss of Mrs. Blossom* prepared her to take on other new roles and images. In her next film, *Two Mules for Sister Sara* (1970), MacLaine played a cigar-smoking, hard-drinking, blasphemous whore, who poses as a nun, teamed against tight-lipped, grizzled-chin Clint Eastwood.

Two Mules for Sister Sara, directed by veteran Don Siegel, opens with an amazing credit sequence (shot by assistant director, Joe Cavalier), which establishes the tone of the film. Filling the techni-colored, wide screen with lions, snakes, and scorpions, Siegel sets forth a barren Mexican terrain. Into this hostile environment rides Hogan (East-wood), arriving just in time to save the almost naked Sara (MacLaine) from three brutish rapists. Hogan discovers with great disappointment that Sara is a nun, devoted to God's work. Begrudgingly, he agrees to help her evade the French army, which is pursuing her because she supports the Mexican revolutionaries known as Juarists. At a ruined fort, Hogan kills a rattlesnake and Sara uses its tail to scare away the French soldiers. Sara's bravery gains Hogan's respect, but he admits that he believes in no causes and, as a mercenary, will help her on a cash basis only.

As the two travel across Mexico in search of funds for the Juarists, Hogan finds himself both attracted to Sister Sara, who demonstrates an unexpected earthy quality, and puzzled by her irreverent behavior and open profanity.

Traveling is slow, as Sara's only means of locomotion is a small mule. Hogan rides his horse. On the way to Chihuahua, where Sara intends to aid in the attack on the French army, Hogan is wounded by an Indian arrow. Sara uses her silver cross as a sun reflector to frighten off the savages and saves the couple for the second time. Sara must then operate on Hogan. Fortified with whiskey, Hogan instructs Sara as she pushes the arrow through his body and cauterizes the wound. Task accomplished, she, too, takes a slug of alcohol.

Their next adventure entails blowing up a bridge to destroy a French supply train. It falls on Sara to scale the supports and plant the dynamite. Overcoming her fear of heights, she successfully performs her job and then finds Hogan too drunk to aim properly. Filled with rage, she screams "Sober up, you bastard." As she slugs him, Hogan shoots and explodes the dynamite, just in the nick of time.

The two continue together to Chihuahua. Here the Mexicans plan to enter the French garrison by way of the neighboring church wall. The attack is set for Bastille Day when the soldiers will be drunk. In Chihuahua, Hogan discovers to his amazement (if not ours), that Sara is really a whore

Two Mules for Sister Sara—with Clint Eastwood.

who has donned holy vestments for self-protection. Before he has time to digest this information, the attack begins. Hogan's skills are put to good use. Meanwhile, Sara sacrifices herself as a prisoner to get inside the garrison. After a long, violent battle, the fort finally falls to the Mexicans.

Hot from fighting, Hogan bursts into Sara's room. He finds her in the bathtub smoking a cigar and plunges in, clothes and all. Sara remarks, "the least you can do is take off your hat." Hogan responds, "No time." The film ends with the two once again in the desert. Sara, again mounted on a mule, is now adorned in a fancy red silk dress and hat, her painted face showing just beneath a black umbrella. Hogan, having won the lady, nonetheless has obvious second thoughts about her collection of hatboxes.

The film was released in June 1970 to fine reviews. Roger Greenspan of *The New York Times* called it a "movie lover's dream." Having directed

Two Mules for Sister Sara—her real identity.

Two Mules for Sister Sara—with Clint Eastwood.

twenty-seven films (and having worked on untold more), Siegel had a strong following among knowledgeable critics, especially those with a taste for male action films. Greenspan also commented on "the exceptional narrative intelligence,"[1] which he attributed to director Budd Boetticher, who was responsible for the original story. Boetticher is noted for a distinguished series of Westerns that he made between 1956 and 1960. The episodic quality of *Two Mules for Sister Sara* is reminiscent of these works, which are structured along the lines of a journey.

Despite the spectacular seige in Chihuahua, skillfully directed by Siegel with 120 separate shots and 70 camera setups,[2] the film is basically a comic-romance for two characters. As such, *Two Mules for Sister Sara* captures much of the spark and spirit of the thirties' male-female comedies directed by Preston Sturges, Howard Hawks, and Frank Capra. In fact, one critic compared it with the Capra classic *It Happened One Night*. The

lively dialogue must be credited to scriptwriter Albert Maltz. (Maltz was blacklisted during the fifties and made his comeback in *Two Mules*.)

Most of the critics commented on the fine performances by both Eastwood and MacLaine and on the stunning photography by Gabriel Figueroa (the Mexican cinematographer who shot Luis Buñuel's *Nazarin, Exterminating Angel,* and *Simon of the Desert*). Writing for *Commonweal*, Richard Corliss stated: "The characters created by Boetticher and Maltz have a resilience and humor perfectly matched by the stars who portray them."[3] However, Jay Cocks of *Time* was not so taken with Eastwood and felt that MacLaine's Sister Sara was hardly an improvement over other recent roles. He said, "Shirley MacLaine . . . has considerable range and some charm, both of which have been pretty well blunted by the monotonous consistency of her roles."[4]

Siegel himself had some reservations about casting MacLaine in the role of Sara. Originally the

158

Two Mules for Sister Sara—MacLaine and Eastwood.

part was intended for Elizabeth Taylor, who wanted to do the role, but Universal preferred MacLaine.[5] (Interestingly, this is the second role Taylor lost to MacLaine. Taylor was the first choice for *Irma la Douce*.)[6] Siegel was not happy with the change. In an interview he stated, "As fine an actress as she is, the map of Ireland is all over her face. The nun was originally supposed to be Mexican. She was cast wrong. It had nothing to do with her talent, but it made it hard for us."[7]

Working was anything but smooth. Although Siegel had high praise for MacLaine's performance, especially in the scene where Sara removes the arrow from Hogan's shoulder, he had difficulty relating to her as a woman. Remembering the problems on location, he said, "There are some women I feel I didn't get along with particularly well. Shirley MacLaine is one. I don't know what she thinks of me, but I know we had one tremendous fight in the wilds of Mexico in which I think we were both wrong. It's hard to feel any great warmth for her. She's too . . . unfeminine. She has too much balls."[8]

Oddly enough, a woman "with balls" is exactly the kind of female that Siegel had portrayed in many of his films. In his male-dominated world, women seldom played a central part. But those who did *(Baby Face Nelson* and *The Killers)* were self-confident broads who were not afraid to take risks or to participate in a man's world. Although Siegel's female characters often turn out to be betrayers, as in *The Killers* and *The Hanged Man* (Sara qualifies as a deceiver rather than a betrayer), these heroines are true equals of their male counterparts. Thus, despite the bad feelings between Siegel and MacLaine, he did capture her athletic energy, easy humor, candor, and resourcefulness, with even a nod to her social commitment.

Siegel sensed MacLaine's strength and transformed it into a fine performance. Sara presented a new challenge for MacLaine — a bold departure from her numerous portrayals as the pathetic victim of the world and the brassy broad played off against a gentle or ineffectual hero. Here, at last, were two characters of equal intelligence and courage, pitted against one another, and forming an alliance against other forces. Sara is the one woman who can hold her own with Hogan, a man who believes that all women are natural born liars and who casually takes women when he wants them. Hogan is confident that he is a member of the stronger sex and fails to realize, until the end, that Sara has led him around by the nose like a mule (thus the film's title). They are a perfect pair. As one critic has noted: "Eastwood's surliness, his skill with and disposition to use dynamite, are contrasted with MacLaine's optimistic, rabid determination to have a part in the assault." Certainly this optimism shines forth from some private source within MacLaine herself.

28

Desperate Characters

Following the sophisticated *Mrs. Blossom* and the earthy *Sister Sara*, MacLaine did a complete turn about by undertaking to help finance and star in a grim tale of life in New York City, written by playwright Frank D. Gilroy *(Days of Wine and Roses, The Only Game in Town)*. Gilroy had tried unsuccessfully to find backing for his screenplay *Desperate Characters*, which he also intended to direct. MacLaine read the script and became so committed to the project that she convinced Sir Lew Grade, head of England's Independent Television Corporation, to put up $320,000 (hardly a handsome sum for a commercial project). To make ends meet, MacLaine also agreed to a percentage of the film in lieu of her usual salary.

The action of *Desperate Characters* (1971) is minimal. The story covers one weekend in the lives of Sophie and Otto Bentwood (MacLaine and Kenneth Mars), a middle-aged couple living in Brooklyn Heights. Otto is a conservative, upper-middle-class attorney. Both are intelligent, bored individuals who wonder what went wrong. Otto protects himself by criticizing others; Sophie masks her feelings by observing rather than participating in life. Their story is told against the background of the New York cityscape — an urban environment filled with fear, suffering, and sudden outbreaks of violence.

The story opens on a Friday evening as the two sit at dinner. The casual conversation does little to hide the repressed tension between them. When Sophie goes out to feed a stray cat she has befriended, it suddenly bites her hand. Ignoring the incident, the two leave for a party. At their friend's apartment, Sophie sees Francis Early, a man with whom she had a six-month affair.

Back at home Sophie has difficulty sleeping. After midnight, Charlie (Gerald O'Loughlin), Otto's law partner, rings the bell. Charlie is upset and hurt by Otto's desire to dissolve their partnership over philosophic differences. Sophie decides not to wake Otto and goes with Charlie for a cup of coffee. For the first time that evening, Sophie openly laughs.

The next day Sophie visits the Museum of Modern Art, where she accidently meets Ruth, Charlie's wife. Ruth is cordial but aloof.

Next, Sophie goes to see her good friend Claire (Sada Thompson). Claire has been divorced for over twenty years but has a sometimes living arrangement with her ex-husband Leon (Jack Somack). Sophie finds their loveless bickering so demeaning that she finally rushes out of the apartment. Lonely and depressed, she calls Francis, but he is in bed with another woman and refuses to answer the telephone.

Back home a black man rings the doorbell, asking permission to use the telephone. Although

Desperate Characters—with Kenneth Mars (far left).

Otto has misgivings, he allows him inside and eventually lends him ten dollars, which he knows will never be returned. Concerned about Sophie's bite, Otto takes her to the hospital for a tetanus shot. The waiting room is filled with screaming and suffering patients. Sophie and Otto are told by the doctor that the cat must be retrieved or Sophie will have to undergo rabies shots. The two return home and finally manage to catch the stray.

Since word on the cat will not come until Monday, Otto suggests they spend Sunday at their summer house. When they arrive in the country, they are horrified to find a filthy, ransacked house, although nothing is missing. They secretly suspect a neighbor whom they believe harbors resentment for the rich New Yorkers who come down for the summer. Frustrated and angry, Otto forces Sophie to make love before they return to the city.

On the way home Otto suggests adopting a baby, but Sophie feels that it is too late for that. As they enter their townhouse, Sophie becomes

fearful and asks, "Suppose they've been here too?" Otto responds, "Not yet," and the two disappear into the darkness.

The world premiere of *Desperate Characters* occurred on 22 September 1971 at the New York Festival Theatre. Later, when the film was shown at the Berlin Film Festival, it won three prizes. The picture received the International Film Critics' award; Gilroy received an award for the best screenplay; and MacLaine took first place as the best actress of the year. The film was subsequently picked up by Paramount Pictures, who had initially turned it down, and distributed commercially. The critics were extremely receptive to *Desperate Characters.* They praised the low-keyed contemporary subject matter and the performances of the stars, and added admiring comments on the accomplishments possible on such a restricted budget. Some voiced reservations about Gilroy's literary dialogue and mannered theatrical direction, but most felt that Gilroy showed promise in his first directorial outing.

New Yorker's Penelope Gilliatt opened her review with a comment on works that reveal a "distaste for the age." She compared *Desperate Characters* with works by Chekhov. "For once, we are in the middle of a New York City-baiting work that is possessed as powerfully as any Chekhov play by the sense that things needn't be so."[1] Noting the film's capacity for revealing the arbitrariness of things, she sums up her feeling by calling the movie an "exquisitely layered film."

Gilliatt's review is representative. There were, however, dissenting opinions. Judith Crist felt the film was an assortment of "current urban clichés," and *The Washington Post's* Gary Arnold found the film "disagreeable" and "heavy-handed." Charles Champlin of *The Los Angeles Times* claimed that "the plot wears more symbols than a Christmas tree."[2]

For MacLaine, however, there was nothing but praise. In addition to her acting ability, the critics highly respected her willingness to accept such an unflattering role (and unflattering camera angles) — and a paycut as well. Champlin said, "Shirley MacLaine is more impressive than I have ever seen her, acting with an intensity, intelligence and maturity which erases even the dimmest trace of the charming kook who came among us years ago."[3] Gilliatt called her performance "a giant stride forward. Other actresses would have been more obvious casting. Shirley MacLaine is surprising in the part, but she is working miles within her resources."[4] And Roger Ebert of *The Chicago Sun-Times* stated that "Shirley MacLaine achieves one of the great performances of the year. She proves that we were right, when we saw her in films like *The Apartment*, to know that she really had it all, could go all the way with a serious role."[5]

Ebert's comment was correct. MacLaine had not played a straight dramatic role since *Two For the*

Desperate Characters—with Gerald O'Loughlin.

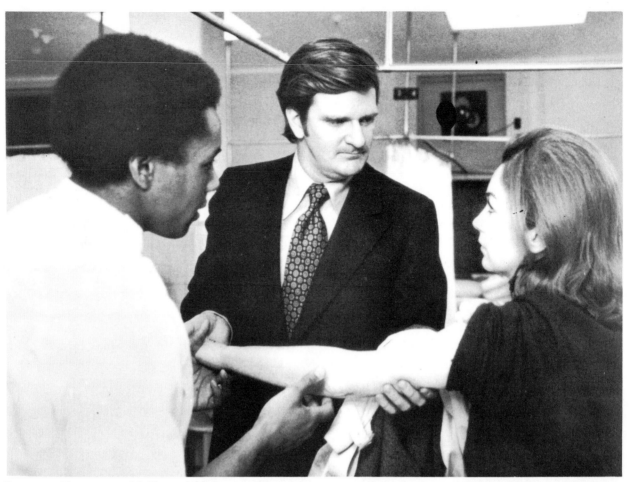

Desperate Characters—with Kenneth Mars.

Desperate Characters

Seesaw in 1962. Since the middle sixties she had been concentrating on her natural talent — comedy — and audiences had forgotten her fine performances in films like *Hot Spell* and *The Children's Hour*. By returning to drama, MacLaine not only had a chance to develop further this side of her personality, but also had a platform on which to comment about the quality of life in this country. *Desperate Characters* reflected MacLaine's growing seriousness, which ultimately led to McGovern's campaign trail in 1972.

Aside from age, resemblances between Shirley and Sophie are almost negligible. Sophie seems almost devoid of any resources. Yet *Desperate Characters* is definitely a woman's film. Both Sophie and Otto represent the film's desperate characters (based on Thoreau's statement "The mass of men lead lives of quiet desperation"), but the center of the work is Sophie. It is she whom we follow from scene to scene and she with whom we identify. The film's vision reflects her inner world, projected outward onto the city. The ugliness portrayed on the screen emmanates from her dissatisfaction and discomfort; the sense of unease, from her own turmoil.

Compared with other movies released in 1971, *Desperate Characters* is unique in offering a female role of such dimensions. Only Jane Fonda's Academy Award winning portrayal of a prostitute in *Klute* (an incursion into MacLaine's territory) can compare. Films like *The French Connection, A Clockwork Orange, Fiddler on the Roof, The Last Picture Show,* and *Nicholas and Alexandra* either relegated women to minor, if interesting, roles, or ignored them altogether.

Desperate Characters, on the other hand, touches on the plight of many women. Sophie, no longer young, finds herself trapped in a marriage long gone sour. Whereas Otto has anesthetized himself to life's problems, Sophie remains sensitive and vulnerable. In her search for answers, Sophie has tried an extramarital affair, but like all other relationships nothing seems nourishing. Sophie's female friends provide no solutions either. Claire is a lonely, castrating woman. Ruth's new reliance on the women's movement has left her committed but unfeeling. Sophie wanders from place to place, secretly suffering but committed to nothing. Though we long for her to burst out and break free, the film offers no easy answers.

Unfortunately, seen today, *Desperate Characters* lacks the impact it had in 1971. Perhaps we have become too accustomed to hearing the cries about urban crisis. Whatever, the film reeks of a social message. The cards seemed stacked; the ugliness, too insistent. We wonder what more can happen in the space of one weekend. Gilroy pushes us to the brink of credibility.

Despite glowing reviews, *Desperate Characters* did not become the commercial success everyone had hoped for. Perhaps the downbeat story was simply too depressing, too familiar (if not totally real). In this film, with no beginning and no ending, there is neither catharsis nor tragedy to purge our emotions and make us whole again. *Desperate Characters* simply stops, leaving us with a sick heart.

29

The Possession of Joel Delaney

Having turned her career in a new direction, MacLaine undertook next a supernatural thriller, *The Possession of Joel Delaney* (1972). Like *Desperate Characters,* the film focused on an attractive, upper-middle-class woman enmeshed in the harrowing experiences of contemporary New York City.

The Possession of Joel Delaney opens at a chic party on Manhattan's Upper East Side. Norah Benson (MacLaine), a divorcée in her late thirties, arrives with her brother Joel (Perry King). The two obviously have a close relationship. The next day Joel takes his niece Carrie (Lisa Kohane) and his nephew Peter (David Elliott) skating. As he twirls Carrie around on the ice his expression gradually becomes sinister. That evening Norah calls Joel, who has moved to his own apartment in a Puerto Rican neighborhood. Alarmed by his groaning response, she rushes to his building as the police carry Joel off to Bellevue Hospital in handcuffs.

Norah returns to his apartment, unable to believe that Joel, normally gentle and reserved, could have attacked the super with a knife. Inside she finds a filthy room filled with many strange religious objects. Hanging on the wall is a large painted hand, drawn by Joel's Puerto Rican friend Tonio Perez. Through the intervention of Norah's ex-husband, a physician, Joel is released from Bellevue in the care of Erika Lorenz (Lovelady Powell), a psychiatrist friend of Norah's.

Erika discovers that Joel, who lives in Tonio's apartment, considers the youth his only real friend and admires him because "he stands for everything Norah hates." Norah, concerned about Joel's health, moves him back into her apartment. But Joel remains moody, and the two argue over her sex life. Unable to remain cooped up, Joel skips out to a party.

A short time later, Norah plans a rather adolescent party in honor of Joel's birthday. Everyone tries to ignore what has happened; however, Joel acts very strangely and then abruptly breaks out into Spanish, scaring the whole family and especially Veronica, the maid.

The next day Norah goes to Sherry, Joel's girlfriend, and is horrified to find her dead body, nude and decapitated. The police believe that the murder is related to three similar cases that have been attributed to Tonio. Joel, deeply upset, breaks into tears. Meanwhile, Norah goes to Spanish Harlem to persuade Veronica to return to work. Reluctant to offer any explanation, Veronica gives Norah the name of a *botanica,* who she says can help. The *botanica,* don Pedro, knows the case and informs Norah that Tonio is dead. He explains that Tonio's spirit has entered Joel's body and must be exorcized. Norah is suspicious and uncomfortable, but she nevertheless agrees to visit

The Possession of Joel Delaney—with Perry King.

don Pedro again. As she makes her way through the streets of El Barrio, these emotions become intensified until she races for a taxi in panic.

Despite a long, frenetic ritual, don Pedro declares the ceremony a failure because Norah does not truly believe. Overwrought, Norah confides her fears to Erika. Erika believes that Joel is sick, not possessed. She recommends that Norah take the children to the beach house until Joel is safely hospitalized.

Norah and the children arrive at the house at night. Norah sleeps fitfully. In the morning she is shocked to find Erika's head in the kitchen. This announces Joel's arrival. Dressed in a black leather jacket and dark glasses, he proceeds to threaten her and the children with a switchblade knife. The police arrive, alerted by Erika's husband, but are forced to bide their time. When Joel begins to harass Carrie and Peter, Norah attacks. Joel grabs Norah and kisses her, then emerges from the house using her as a shield. He is shot down by the police.

As Norah rocks the dead body in her arms, a strange look slowly crosses her face. Picking up Joel's knife, she opens it with a new fascination.

Like *Desperate Characters*, *The Possession of Joel Delaney* was produced by Independent Television Corporation as part of a deal MacLaine had made with Sir Lew Grade. Like *Desperate Characters*, the film was shot on location in New York City. However, despite the popular potential of a contemporary horror film, *The Possession of Joel Delaney* fared no better at the box office than its predecessor, and it received decidedly worse reviews.

Judith Crist's reaction in *New York* magazine summed up the responses of other critics: "The Matt Robinson-Grimes Grice elliptical screenplay and Waris Hussein's pedestrian direction, however, turn it into a lurid web of confused implications that suddenly collapses into a mass of absurdities that are underscored by the realities of the New York locations in which the film was prettily

The Possession of Joel Delaney—with Lisa Kohane.

photographed."[1] Although Waris Hussein had
sparked interest with his 1970 offbeat comedy
*Quackser Fortune Has a Cousin in the Bronx, The
Possession of Joel Delaney* left critics cold.

One or two critics did respond to a disturbing
element in the film that indicated that *Joel
Delaney* might be more than a routine horror
story. Arthur Knight, writing for *The Saturday
Review,* protested against the negative stereotyping
of the Puerto Ricans, which he felt portrayed them
as "sly, secretive, psychotic voodoo worshipers."[2]
Responding to similar factors, but from another
perspective, Andrew Sarris in *The Village Voice*
commented that "under the surface of this uncon-
vincing grand guignol is the first film testament to
the palpable tension between the ruling classes on
Manhattan's East Side and the Puerto Rican
subjects in El Barrio." [3] To a large degree we
experience the film from Norah's point of view,
and there is little doubt that, from her seemingly

secure position, the Puerto Ricans are an alien
culture — mysterious and threatening.

The only unqualified praise for *The Possession
of Joel Delaney* went to MacLaine. *Variety*
referred to MacLaine's "riveting performance," and
Knight called her acting "strikingly taut." *The Los
Angeles Times* was even more specific, taking time
to indicate the new direction of MacLaine's career.
"With *The Possession of Joel Delaney,* Shirley
MacLaine continues an exciting new phase in her
career that began with *Desperate Characters.* Gone
is the vulnerable, irresistible hoyden image that all
those hookers-with-a-heart-of-gold parts gave her,
and in its place is the sophisticated, canny woman,
beautiful yet mature, that is lots closer to the real
Miss MacLaine."[4]

The Times may be right that MacLaine's depic-
tion of a "sophisticated, canny woman" was "lots
closer to the real Miss MacLaine" than her "vulnerable, irresistible hoyden image," but the critic,

The Possession of Joel Delaney

Kevin Thomas, was obviously overlooking several aspects of Norah's personality.

In many ways the role of Norah echoes common characteristics already developed in Sophie *(Desperate Characters)*. It is to MacLaine's credit that she would undertake two such unflattering roles. Both are upper-middle-class women who live in the comfortable luxury of New York City, surrounded by a hostile world that eventually begins to close in on them within the sanctity of their own homes. Both are frustrated and dissatisfied. Sophie borders on the brink of self-knowledge, although she lacks the courage to act on her own convictions. Norah, smug in her posh apartment, surrounded by material possessions, blinds herself to any hint of disturbance.

Both films smack of Hollywood's traditional treatment of the middle-aged woman — one that portrays her as sexually frustrated, hysterical, and usually a spinster. Marjorie Rosen has pointed out

the tendency, especially in the fifties, to portray the older Woman Alone as half a person.[5] Technically, neither Sophie nor Norah is actually alone, but both suffer from unsatisfactory sexual relationships, and both appear emotionally crippled: Sophie in her passive, comatose state; Norah by her childish, spoiled manner. Thus, a hint of misogyny hovers over the portrayals of both women, which differs little from the films of the fifties.

In many ways misogyny constitutes a standard element in most horror films from the days of *Dracula* and *Frankenstein* to the modern stories by Alfred Hitchcock. Women in horror movies are inevitably the victims — usually the beautiful prey of some ugly or pernicious monster. In Hitchcock thrillers, women, often blond and beautiful, suffer physical harm or psychological intimidation *(Dial M For Murder, Rear Window, Vertigo, Psycho, The Birds, Frenzy,* and others). Sexual overtones are rampant throughout horror films — from vampires who attack sleeping beauties to hairy apes who strip helpless heroines. As the weaker sex, women serve as convenient objects upon which to perpetrate a crime.

The Possession of Joel Delaney clearly falls within the category of a horror thriller. And Wanda Hale in her review of *Desperate Characters* referred to the movie as a "downbeat horror story." All of the elements are there. In both films the heroine moves from one harrowing experience to another. In *Desperate Characters* these events end in a forcible rape, which allows Otto to vent his angry feelings upon Sophie. In *The Possession of Joel Delaney*, the film ends just short of Norah's sexual humiliation and decapitation at the hands of Joel.

30

The Other Half of the Sky: A China Memoir

In 1971, while attending a diplomatic reception, MacLaine received an open invitation to visit the People's Republic of China. This welcome was extended by Chiao Kuan Hua, the Chinese foreign minister, in hopes that such a trip would help Americans understand better what China had accomplished in the past forty years. A true statesman, Kuan Hua was not oblivious to the influence movie stars have on American public opinion.

Two years later this casual invitation became a reality. Heading a group of twelve, MacLaine led the first American Women's Delegation to China. She followed instructions from the Chinese government, carefully selecting a cross-section of "regular" Americans. The group included Unita Blackwell, a black civil-rights worker from Mississippi; Patricia Branson, a southern George Wallace supporter who worked as a clerk; Rosa Marin, a sociologist from the University of Puerto Rico; Ninibah Crawford, an American Indian who lived in a trailer with her children on the Navaho reservation; Margaret Whitman, a conservative Republican from Long Island; Phyllis Kronhausen, a psychologist and author of several books on sexology; and Karine Boutilier, a twelve-year-old student from Racine, Wisconsin, who had organized a boycott for the United Farm Union.

MacLaine had also secured permission to include a four-member, all-women's crew to film the group's confrontation with the mysterious East. After twenty years of facing the cameras, MacLaine relished the opportunity of making a film of her own.

The crew was headed by Claudia Weill, a twenty-eight-year-old documentary filmmaker. Her early short *This is the Home of Mrs. Levant Graham* (1970) had won the grand prix at the Ann Arbor Film Festival. She also served as cinematographer on *Year of the Woman*, a feature-length documentary filmed at the 1972 Democratic Convention. Assisting Claudia were Nancy Shreiber, a twenty-four-year-old electrician; Cabell Smith, a thirty-year-old NBC sound technician (and the only woman in the New York union); and Joan Weidman, a twenty-two-year-old camerawoman and assistant director.

The delegation left New York on 16 April 1973 for three weeks in a foreign world. Lugging two-thousand pounds of equipment and one-hundred-thousand feet of film, they set out to discover the unknown. The film, *The Other Half of the Sky: A China Memoir*, documents what the women found, saw, and felt. It also deals with the interactions within the group. According to Weill, the film was not "a documentary about China, but

The American Women's Delegation with their Chinese hosts—China, 1973.

China through what we could see of it ... a document of two cultures looking at each other."[1]

After a prologue, which introduces each member in her own home, China is initially viewed through the window of a moving train. Outside are huge, colorful, revolutionary billboards and the round, happy faces of singing children. Everywhere there are clean, emaculate streets filled only with the ubiquitous bicycles.

The following seventy-four minutes show the women attending briefings by the people's revolutionary committee and then visiting an average Chinese family, a nursery school, the big May Day event at T'ien Men Square (graced by the appearance of Madame Chou En Lai), an art workshop, a commune outside of Shanghai, and, finally, a hospital to watch a Cesarian section performed with acupuncture.

Unanimously, the women sensed a great personal calm and happiness among all the people they met. After hearing about the hardships and injustices of prerevolutionary China, they could appreciate the enormous accomplishments of the People's Republic — fundamental changes that affected not only economics and politics but also attitudes towards women. The group was touched by the gentle kindness of everyone and surprised by their shy, almost Puritanic attitudes towards personal matters. Claudia Weill pointed out that in China women are strong, tender, and possess a sense of humor — qualities that seem contradictory in our society.

The group was more ambivalent in responding to the noncompetitive, uniform quality of Chinese life. MacLaine found it difficult to accept a philosophy that has no place for a unique, creative talent like Michelangelo and which appropriates all art for state purposes.

At the East-Is-Red Nursery School the view of Chinese education ellicited varied reactions from the women. All respected the group spirit and sense of sharing. Pat Branson admired an attitude that fostered "pride of work." But Margaret

Whitman was appalled at what appeared to her as programmed children.

Shaken, moved, and exhausted, the group returned to America. MacLaine, Weill, and Aviva Slesin, a New York editor, immediately began turning fifty hours of film into a feature documentary that would honestly reflect their unique experience. MacLaine wrote the narration; Weill and Slesin edited. The project took over nine months to complete. It was premiered at the 1974 Cannes Film Festival and, although it drew much interest and provoked much controversy, MacLaine was not able to find a commercial distributor who wanted a film about women in a far-off country called China. Backing had come from Frank Yablans, the former president of Paramount Pictures (with additional sums from MacLaine herself), but Paramount was not interested in handling such an offbeat subject.

Anxious for Americans to see the film, Mac-Laine worked out a deal with the Public Broadcasting System. *The Other Side of the Sky* was finally aired on 15 April 1975, a full two years after the trip. Subsequently it was nominated for an Oscar as the best documentary of 1975 but lost out to *Hearts and Minds.*

The film also screened briefly at the Whitney Museum in March 1975, provoking diverse reactions. Many were favorable. Marjorie Rosen, reviewing for *Ms.* magazine, claimed that as an introduction to China it was "the purest and most frankly emotional exploration I've seen."[2] *Newsweek* warned that it would "disturb some who cling to preconceived ideas about China," calling the documentary "an intensely moving leap forward into a society whose values are so different from our own."[3]

Others were not so moved. *The Village Voice* critic Molly Haskell found the sentiments expressed repugnant to her concepts of freedom and individuality. She balked at conditioned responses, learning by rote, and idealization of the masses. She stated: "If the purpose of the film is . . . to offer 'insight into the universal qualities

MacLaine meets Madame Chou En Lai.

that are part of human nature and cross the boundaries of race, culture, and politics,' its effect was quite the opposite on me."[4]

Perhaps most damning were the accusations of O. Edmund Clubb and Walter Goodman. Clubb, a China expert and invited guest on the television preview, implied that the women, including MacLaine, were politically naive, buying the propaganda China wanted to sell. Goodman, writing on the pages of the *The New York Times*, accused MacLaine of using pure propaganda to advance a cause.

Two weeks later MacLaine responded to these charges, also in *The New York Times*. Starting with the proposition that all works of art forward some cause, she pointed out the ways in which our government also uses propaganda and how our schools program our children. MacLaine recognized the weakness of a defense based on "others do it too" and, therefore, drew a distinction between malignant and constructive propaganda. Next she questioned whether filming what she actually saw constituted patronization of the Chinese. Finally she stated:

> But for now, judging from my own experience which I tried to capture on film, there is something going on in China that is quite important, certainly worth seeing and hopefully worth understanding. I mean one of the largest experiments in social organization in modern history.[5]

The Chinese experience as depicted in *The Other Half of the Sky* proved to be only half of the story. Revitalized by her journey, MacLaine returned to America and proceeded to elaborate on her thoughts and feelings in a second autobiography, *You Can Get There From Here*. The book chronicles the agonizing experience of filming *Shirley's World* and moves on to the exhilarating and then frustrating months campaigning with Senator George McGovern. However, the main body of the book is devoted to China.

You Can Get There From Here reveals the tensions behind the scenes, the homesickness, the culture shock, the temper tantrums, and the physical discomfort of MacLaine and the eleven women. Naturally, it expresses only her point of view. Perceptively MacLaine admits, "Every journey in which more than one person takes part becomes 'Rashomon,' and I suppose each of the women would have a different version of what actually happened."[6]

But despite her own disappointments, MacLaine left China with a new lease on life. For her the lesson of China is that we can still hope. The book ends with MacLaine's return to herself. She says, "A week later, I walked into a dance studio for the first time in twenty years."[7]

174

31

The Turning Point

After a five-year hiatus filled with television specials, live performances, political campaigns, a disastrous television series, a trip to China, one documentary film and a second autobiography, MacLaine returned to the cameras in Herbert Ross's *The Turning Point* (1977).

In *The Turning Point* MacLaine returned full circle to the world of ballet where she had begun. The film highlights the joys and pains of this special world—the jealousies, the aching muscles, the endless classes, and the sacrifices (although not sexual), all of which seem to vanish in that magical moment when the dancer steps out onto the stage. Ross and screenwriter Arthur Laurents even capture the small details of a dancer's life—the ugly feet, the penguin walk, sewing ribbons on toe shoes, and the adulating pupils who crowd at the practice-room door to glimpse their favorite star. In addition, the film offers a package of gems from such classical works as *Giselle, Don Quixote, Romeo and Juliet,* and *Bayadére.*

The film marked the acting debut of Russian superstar, ballet danseur, Mikhail Baryshnikov. As such it was anxiously awaited by balletomanes around the world, rivaled only by Rudolph Nureyev's debut in *Valentino.* As his dancing partner and romantic love, the languid Gelsey Kirkland was cast opposite Baryshnikov. But days before shooting began, Kirkland suffered an injury and had to be replaced by Leslie Browne.

The movie concerns the lives of four ballet dancers played by MacLaine, Anne Bancroft, Mikhail Baryshnikov, and Leslie Browne. MacLaine and Bancroft play two aging dancers, each of whom has chosen a different life. MacLaine decided to have a family and has become an Oklahoma City housewife. Bancroft, having chosen a career over love and marriage, is now facing a professional decline.

The two actresses, in outstanding, highly emotional performances, portray fully developed, mature women on the brink of middle age. Each reflects back on her life and questions whether she has made the right choices. Neither is totally satisfied, but both conclude that basically they have each followed the right path and that each alternative provides its own rewards and disappointments.

The two characters are a study in contrast, and together they are explosive. As Deedee, MacLaine exudes warmth, emotion, and a casual openness. As Emma, Bancroft appears just the opposite—controlled, dignified, self-assured. In a magnificent scene toward the end of the film, the two women confront one another with words and physical assaults. As they slug it out, Deedee reveals the doubts and jealousies that have plagued her for seventeen years, the regrets of having abandoned her career. Emma admits to the insatiable ambition that drove her to become a prima ballerina at any

The Turning Point

cost and to the knowledge that despite an unpromising future from here on in, she'd make the same choice over again. The scene is dramatically cathartic and refreshingly honest.

The central focus of the film is on the younger dancers, Yuri (Baryshnikov) and MacLaine's daughter, Emilia (Browne). Emilia is a talented seventeen-year-old member of the *corps de ballet* who is in love with Yuri. Like her mother, she must now choose between a life of dedication, which excludes all but dance, or marriage in which her career aspirations will be secondary.

When Emilia discovers Yuri with another ballerina and realizes that his attentions are fleeting, she finds little difficulty in coming to a conclusion. Thus the turning point has arrived, and the decision has been made.

The film opened in October 1977 to unanimous praise and predictions of many awards. By January 1978 it had already picked up a Golden Globe as the year's best dramatic motion picture. *Variety* stated, "*The Turning Point* is one of the best films of this era. It's that rare example of synergy in

The Turning Point—with Anne Bancroft

The Turning Point—with Leslie Browne

which every key element is excellent and the ensemble is an absolute triumph."[1]

In February MacLaine received her fourth Academy Award nomination for her role as Deedee. In addition, *The Turning Point* picked up ten other Oscar nominations.

Although different critics voiced different minor complaints, most notably the lack of integration of the dance sequences into the narrative whole or Leslie Browne's icy performance, almost all agreed that here at last were two female stars that could hold their own against the Newman-Redford, Hoffman-McQueen, or Caine-Connery charisma.

Released amid a stream of "women's pictures" such as *Looking for Mr. Goodbar, You Light Up My Life,* and *Julia* (which offered another powerful duo—Jane Fonda and Vanessa Redgrave), *The Turning Point* became part of Hollywood's attempt to catch up with the changing times and the new life-styles and aspirations of females throughout America. Many critics with a feminist consciousness were delighted to find a film that finally, according to *The Village Voice*'s Andrew Sarris,

countered "Hollywood's traditional middle-class prejudice in favor of congugality over careerism. "[2] Perceptively Molly Haskell, writing for *New York* magazine, concluded, "The balance would be overwhelmingly in favor of the career woman were it not for Shirley MacLaine's magnificence in the role of the Oklahoma City housewife.... She makes motherhood and family a living, breathing thing instead of a sitcom."[3]

The roles played by MacLaine and Bancroft provide a rare contemporary recognition of the hundreds of talented career women in America (some in the arts, many in other fields).

Although female news reporters, pianists, and even fliers were movie staples in the 1930s and 1940s, few such women have graced the screen in recent years. And unlike Katharine Hepburn in *Woman of the Year* or Rosalind Russell in *His Girl Friday, The Turning Point* does not end with a reconciliation and female capitulation. However, it should be noted that only the woman is presented with the either/or proposition. Clearly, Yuri would not be called upon to make such a choice. Even as a dedicated artist, he can have his cake and eat it

The Turning Point—with Anne Bancroft

The Turning Point—with Leslie Browne and Anne Bancroft

too—dance and have a wife. Only Emilia must sacrifice one aspect of her life for another. As Emma had stated earlier in the film, if she were a male dancer she could have had all the children she wanted and still danced.

As director, Herbert Ross was an eminently logical choice. Having worked as a ballet-company and movie choreographer, he was not only intimate with the world of dance, but also personally aware of its problems. Further, as husband of Nora Kaye, for many years prima ballerina of Ballet Theatre, he had firsthand knowledge of the special demands placed upon female dancers, which is an integral part of *The Turning Point*.

The idea of sacrifice and tragic love are also themes that occur in earlier Ross productions such as *Funny Girl* (1968), *Goodbye, Mr. Chips* (1969), *Play it Again, Sam* (1972), and *Funny Lady* (1975). Likewise, Arthur Laurents, whose career dates back to the 1940s, has written a classic, bittersweet love story with many of the same overtones as his *The Way We Were* (1975).

It is doubtful that *The Turning Point* will be MacLaine's last film. In typical MacLaine fashion, there is always something brewing in the pot. No doubt, this film will simply be another turning point in her already fascinating career.

Filmography

The Trouble with Harry (1955)

Director and Producer: Alfred Hitchcock
Asst. Director: Howard Joslin
Screenplay: John Michael Hayes; based on the novel by Jack Trevor Story
Photography: Robert Burks, A.S.C.
Special Effects: John P. Fulton
Assoc. Producer: Herbert Coleman
Editor: Alma Macrorie
Set Decoration: Hal Pereira, John Goodman, Sam Comer, and Emile Kuri
Music: Bernard Herrmann and Raymond Scott
Song: "Flaggin' the Train to Tuscaloosa"
Lyrics: Mack David
Costumes: Edith Head
Color Consultant: Richard Mueller

VistaVision and Technicolor
Running Time: 99 Minutes
Paramount Pictures

CAST

Capt. Albert Wiles . . . . Edmund Gwenn
Sam Marlowe . . . . John Forsythe
Jennifer Rogers . . . . Shirley MacLaine
Miss Gravely . . . . .Mildred Natwick
Mrs. Wiggs . . . . .Mildred Dunnock
Arnie Rogers . . . . .Jerry Mathers
Calvin Wiggs . . . . Royal Dano
Millionaire . . . . Parker Fennelly
Tramp . . . . Barry Macollum
Dr. Greenbow . . . . .Dwight Marfield
Art Critic .Leslie Woolf
Harry Worp . . . . .Philip Truex
Chauffeur . . . . Ernest Curt Bach

Artists and Models (1955)

Director: Frank Tashlin
Producer: Hal B. Wallis

Asst. Director: C. C. Coleman, Jr.
Screenplay: Frank Tashlin, Hal Kanter and Herbert Parker;
based on the play *Rockabye Baby* by Michael Davidson and
Norman Lessing
Adaptation: Don McGuire
Photography: Daniel L. Fapp
Special Effects: John P. Fulton and Farciot Edouart
Assoc. Producer: Paul Nathan
Costumes: Edith Head
Music: Walter Scharf
Choreography: Charles O'Curran
Songs: Harry Warren and Jack Brooks

Vision and Technicolor
Running Time: 109 Minutes
Paramount Pictures

CAST

Rick Todd	Dean Martin
Eugene Fullstack	Jerry Lewis
Bessie Sparrowbush	Shirley MacLaine
Abigail Parker	Dorothy Malone
Mr. Murdock	Eddie Mayehoff
Sonia	Eva Gabor
Anita	Anita Ekberg
Richard Stilton	George (Foghorn) Winslow
Ivan	Jack Elam
Secret Service Chief Samuels	Herbert Rudley
Secret Service Agent Rogers	Richard Shannon
Secret Service Agent Peters	Richard Webb
Otto	Allan Lee
Kurt	Otto Waldis
Mrs. Milldoon	Kathleen Freeman
Art Baker	Himself
Kelly	Emory Parnell
Colonel Drury	Carleton Young
Specialty Dancer	Nick Castle

and

Margaret Barstow, Martha Wentworth, Sara Berner, Steven
Geray, Ralph Dumke, Clancy Cooper, Charles Evans,
Mortimer Dutra, Frank Jenks, Mide Ross, Ann McCrea,
Patti Ross, Glen Walters, Larri Thomas, Sharon Baird, Eve
Meyer, Dale Hartleben, Mickey Little, Patricia Morrow, Sue
Carlton, Tommy Summer, Max Power, Frances Lansing,
Don Corey, Frank Carter, Dorothy Gordon, Rudy Makoul,
Jeanette Miller

Around the World in 80 Days (1956)

Producer: Michael Todd
Director: Michael Anderson
Screenplay: S. J. Perelman, James Poe, John Farrow; based
on the novel by Jules Verne
Choreography: Paul Godkin
Music: Victor Young
Photography: Lionel Lindon
Art Direction: James Sullivan
Set Decoration: Ross Dowd
Special Effects: Lee Kavitz
Unit Manager: Frank Fox
Costumes: Miles White
Sound: Joseph Kane
Prologue: George Melies

Associate Producers: William Cameron Menzies, Kevin
O'Donovan McClory
Vice President and General Manager: Percy Guth
Executive Assistant: Samuel Lambert
Todd-AO Consultant: Schuyler A. Sanford
Unit Manager: Frank Fox
Screen Credits Designer: Saul Bass

Todd-AO Process and Eastman Color
Running Time: 178 Minutes
United Artists

CAST

Phileas Fogg	David Niven
Passepartout	Cantinflas
Princess Aouda	Shirley MacLaine
Inspector Fix	Robert Newton
Members of the Reform Club	Robert Morley
	Trevor Howard
	Finlay Currie
	Basil Sydney
	Ronald Squires

and

Charles Boyer, Joe E. Brown, Martine Carol, John Carra-
dine, Charles Coburn, Ronald Colman, Melville Cooper,
Noel Coward, Reginald Denny, Andy Devine, Marlene
Dietrich, Luis Miguel Dominguin, Fernandel, Sir John
Gielgud, Hermione Gingold, Jose Greco, Sir Cedric Hard-
wicke, Glynis Johns, Buster Keaton, Evelyn Keyes, Beatrice
Lillie, Peter Lorre, Edmund Lowe, Victor McLaglen, Col.
Tim McCoy, A.E. Matthews, Mike Mazurki, John Mills,
Alan Mowbray, Edward R. Murrow, Jack Oakie, George
Raft, Gilbert Roland, Cesar Romero, Frank Sinatra, Red
Skelton, Richard Wattis, Harcourt Williams

Hot Spell (1958)

Director: Daniel Mann
Producer: Hal B. Wallis
Screenplay: James Poe; based on a play by Lonnie Coleman
Photography: Loyal Griggs
Art Direction: Hal Pereira and Tambi Larsen
Process Photography: Farciot Edouart
Special Photographic Effects: John P. Fulton
Set Decoration: Sam Comer and Arthur Krams
Editor: Warren Low
Costumes: Edith Head
Makeup: Wally Westmore
Hairstyles: Nellie Manley
Asst. Director: Michael D. Moore
Sound: Harold Lewis and Winston Leverett
Music: Alex North
Assoc. Producer: Paul Nathan

VistaVision
Running Time: 86 Minutes
Paramount Pictures

CAST

Alma Duval	Shirley Booth
Jack Duval	Anthony Quinn
Virginia Duval	Shirley MacLaine
Buddy Duval	Earl Holliman
Fan	Eileen Heckart
Billy Duval	Clint Kimbrough
Wyatt	Warren Stevens
Dora May	Jody Lawrence
Harry	Harlan Warde
Ruby	Valerie Allen
Essie Mae	Irene Tedrow
Preacher	Anthony Jochim
Librarian	Elsie Waller

and

Stafford Repp, Bill Walker, Louise Franklin, Johnny Lee, Len Hendry, John Indrisano, Watson H. Downs, William Duray, Tony Merrill and Fred Zendar

The Sheepman (1958)

Director: George Marshall
Producer: Edmund Grainger
Screenplay: William Bowers and James Edward Grant; Adaptation by William Roberts; based on a story by James Edward Grant
Music: Jeff Alexander
Photography: Robert Bronner
Art Direction: William A. Horning and Malcolm Brown
Set Decoration: Henry Grace and Hugh Hunt
Color Consultant: Charles K. Hagedon
Asst. Director: Al Jennings
Editor: Ralph E. Winters
Recording Supervisor: Dr. Wesley C. Miller
Costumes: Walter Plunkett
Makeup: William Tuttle
Hairstyles: Sydney Guilaroff

CinemaScope. Metrocolor
Running Time: 85 Minutes
Metro-Goldwyn-Mayer Pictures

CAST

Jason Sweet	Glenn Ford
Dell Payton	Shirley MacLaine
Johnny Bledsoe (Alias Colonel Stephen Bedford)	Leslie Nielsen
Jumbo McCall	Mickey Shaughnessy
Milt Masters	Edgar Buchanan
Mr. Payton	Willis Bouchey
Choctaw	Pernell Roberts
Marshall	Slim Pickens
Red	Buzz Henry
Angelo	Pedro Gonzales Gonzales

The Matchmaker (1958)

Director: Joseph Anthony
Producer: Don Hartman
Screenplay: John Michael Hayes; based on the play by Thornton Wilder
Photography: Charles Lang, Jr.
Art Direction: Hal Pereira and Roland Anderson
Special Photographic Effects: John P. Fulton
Set Decoration: Sam Comer and Robert Benton
Dialogue Coach: William Ross
Costumes: Edith Head
Editor: Howard Smith
Asst. Director: C.C. Coleman, Jr.
Makeup: Wally Westmore
Hairstyles: Nellie Manley
Sound Recording: Gene Merritt and Winston Leverett
Music: Adolph Deutsch

VistaVision
Running Time: 101 Minutes
Paramount Pictures

CAST

Dolly Levi	Shirley Booth
Cornelius Hackl	Anthony Perkins
Irene Molloy	Shirley MacLaine
Horace Vandergelder	Paul Ford
Barnaby Tucker	Robert Morse
Minnie Fay	Perry Wilson
Malachi Stack	Wallace Ford
Joe Scanion	Russell Collins
August	Rex Evans
Rudolph	Gavin Gordon
Maitre D'	Torbin Meyer

Some Came Running (1958)

Director: Vincente Minnelli
Producer: Sol C. Siegel
Screenplay: John Patrick and Arthur Sheekman; based on the novel by James Jones
Photography: William H. Daniels
Music: Elmer Bernstein
Art Direction: William A. Horning and Urie McCleary
Set Decoration: Henry Grace and Robert Priestley
Color Consultant: Charles K. Hagedon
Song: "To Love and Be Loved" by Sammy Cahn and James Van Heusen

Editor: Adrienne Fazan
Asst. Director: William McGarry
Sound: Franklin Milton
Costumes: Walter Plunkett
Makeup: William Tuttle

CinemaScope Metrocolor
Running Time: 134 Minutes
Principal Location Scenes Filmed in Madison, Indiana
Metro-Goldwyn-Mayer Pictures

CAST

Dave Hirsh . . . . Frank Sinatra
Bama Dillert . . . . Dean Martin
Ginny Moorhead . . . . Shirley MacLaine
Gwen French . . . . .Martha Hyer
Frank Hirsh . . . . .Arthur Kennedy
Edith Barclay .Nancy Gates
Agnes Hirsh . . . . .Leora Dana
Dawn Hirsch . . . . .Betty Lou Keim
Prof. Robert Haven French . . . . Larry Gates
Raymond Lanchak . . . . Steven Peck
Rosalie . . . . Carmen Phillips
Jane Barclay . . . . .Connie Gilchrist
Smitty . . . . Ned Wever
Wally Dennis . . . . .John Brennan

Ask Any Girl (1959)

Director: Charles Walters
Producer: Joe Pasternak
Screenplay: George Wells; based on the novel by Winifred Wolfe
Music Conducted and Background Score Composed by Jeff Alexander
Song: "I'm In the Mood for Love"
Music: Jimmy McHugh
Lyrics: Dorothy Fields
Photography: Robert Bronner
Art Direction: William A. Horning and Henry Grace
Special Effects: Robert R. Hoag
Editor: John McSweeney, Jr.
Recording Supervisor: Franklin Milton
Costumes: Helen Rose
Color Consultant: Charles K. Hagedon
Asst. Director: Al Jennings
Asst. to the Producer: Irving Aaronson
Hairstyles: Sydney Guilaroff
Makeup: William Tuttle

CinemaScope Metrocolor
Running Time: 98 Minutes
A Euterpe Production
Metro-Goldwyn-Mayer Pictures

CAST

Miles Doughton . . . . David Niven
Meg Wheeler . . . . Shirley MacLaine
Evan Doughton . . . . Gig Young
Ross Taford . . . . .Rod Taylor
Mr. Maxwell . . . . .Jim Backus
Lisa . . . . Claire Kelly
Jeannie Boyden . . . . Elisabeth Fraser
Terri Richards . . . . .Dody Heath
Bert . . . . Read Morgan

Cigarette Sampler . . . . .Mickey Shaughnessy
Refined Young Lady . . . . Carmen Phillips
Hotel Manager . . . . .Helen Wallace
Girls . . . Myrna Hansen, Kasey Rogers, Carrol Byron, Norma French, and Kathy Reed

Career (1959)

Director: Joseph Anthony
Producer: Hal B. Wallis
Screenplay: James Lee; based on his play
Photography: Joseph La Shelle
Assoc. Producer: Paul Nathan
Music: Franz Waxman
Art Direction: Hal Pereira and Walter Tyler
Special Photographic Effects: John P. Fulton

Process Photography: Farciot Edouart
Editor: Warren Low
Song: (Love is A) "Career" by Sammy Cahn and James Van Heusen
Costumes: Edith Head
Set Decoration: Sam Comer and Arthur Krams
Makeup: Wally Westmore
Asst. Director: D. Michael Moore
Hairstyles: Nellie Manley
Sound: Gene Merritt and Winston Leverett

Running Time: 105 Minutes
Paramount Pictures

CAST

Sam Lawson	Anthony Franciosa
Maury Novak	Dean Martin
Sharon Kensington	Shirley MacLaine
Shirley Drake	Carolyn Jones
Barbara	Joan Blackman
Robert Kensington	Robert Middleton
Marjorie Burke	Donna Douglas
Allan Burke	Jerry Paris
Charlie	Frank McHugh
Eric Peters	Chuck Wassil
Shirley's Secretary	Mary Treen
Matt Helmsley	Alan Hewitt
Columnist	Marjorie Bennett

Can-Can (1960)

Director: Walter Lang
Producer: Jack Cummings
Screenplay: Dorothy Kingsley and Charles Lederer; based on the musical comedy by Abe Burrows
Photography: William H. Daniels
Assoc. Producer: Saul Chaplin
Costumes: Irene Sharaff
Art Direction: Lyle R. Wheeler and Jack Martin Smith
Set Decorations: Walter M. Scott and Paul S. Fox
Editor: Robert Simpson
Asst. Director: Joseph E. Rickards
Makeup: Ben Nye
Hairstyles: Myrl Stoltz
Styling Consultant: Tony Duquette
Sound: W.D. Flick and Fred Hynes
Titles Designed by Tom Keogh
Color Consultant: Leonard Doss

Todd-AO Process and Technicolor
A Suffolk-Cummings Production
Running Time: 134 Minutes
Twentieth Century-Fox Pictures

CAST

Francois Durnais	Frank Sinatra
Simone Pistache	Shirley MacLaine
Paul Barriere	Maurice Chevalier
Philippe Forrestier	Louis Jourdan
Claudine	Juliet Prowse
Andre, Headwaiter	Marcel Dalio
Orchestra Leader	Leon Belasco
Bailiff	Nestor Paiva
Photographer	John A. Neris

Judge Merceaux	Jean Del Val
Chevrolet	Eugene Borgen
Recorder	Jonathan Kidd
Severe Woman	Ann Codee
Adam	Marc Wilder

The Apartment (1960)

Producer and Director: Billy Wilder
Screenplay: Billy Wilder and I.A.L. Diamond
Photography: Joseph La Shelle
Art Direction: Alexander Trauner
Set Decorations: Edward G. Boyle
Music: Adolph Deutsch; "Lonely Room" by Adolph Deutsch; "Jealous Lover" by Charles Williams
Editor: Daniel Mandell
Sound: Fred Lau
Makeup: Harry Ray
Assoc. Producers: I.A.L. Diamond and Doane Harrison

Panavision
Running Time: 125 Minutes
The Mirisch Company
United Artists Corporation

CAST

C.C. Baxter	Jack Lemmon
Fran Kubelik	Shirley MacLaine
J.D. Sheldrake	Fred MacMurray
Mr. Dobisch	Ray Walston
Miss Olsen	Edie Adams
Margie MacDougall	Hope Holiday
Dr. Dreyfuss	Jack Kruschen
Mr. Kirkeby	David Lewis
Sylvia	Joan Shawlee
Karl Matuschka	Johnny Seven
Mrs. Dreyfuss	Naomi Stevens
Mrs. Lieberman	Frances Weintraub Lax
The Blonde	Joyce Jameson
Mr. Vanderhof	Willard Waterman
Mr. Eichelberger	David White
The Bartender	Benny Burt
The Santa Claus	Hal Smith

Ocean's Eleven (1960)

Director and Producer: Lewis Milestone
Screenplay: Harry Brown and Charles Lederer; based on a story by George Clayton Johnson and Jack Golden Russell
Photography: William H. Daniels
Art Direction: Nicolai Remisoff
Set Decoration: Howard Bristol
Editor: Philip W. Anderson
Sound: M.A. Merrick
Music Composed and Conducted by Nelson Riddle
Songs by Sammy Cahn and James Van Heusen: "Ain't That A Kick In The Head" (sung by Dean Martin); "EE-O-LEVEN" (sung by Sammy Davis, Jr.)
Costumes: Howard Shoup
Assoc. Producers: Henry W. Sanicola and Milton Ebbins

Asst. to the Producer: Richard Benedict
Production Manager: Jack R. Berne
Orchestrations: Arthur Morton
Titles Designed by Saul Bass
Makeup: Gordon Bau
Asst. Director: Ray Gosnell, Jr.

Panavision. Technicolor
Running Time: 127 Minutes
Location scenes filmed in Las Vegas, Nevada
Warner Bros.

CAST

Danny Ocean	Frank Sinatra
Sam Harmon	Dean Martin
Josh Howard	Sammy Davis, Jr.
Jimmy Foster	Peter Lawford
Beatrice Ocean	Angie Dickinson
Anthony Bergdorf	Richard Conte
Duke Santos	Cesar Romero
Adele Ekstrom	Patrice Wymore
"Mushy" O'Connors	Joey Bishop
Spyros Acebos	Akim Tamiroff

and

Roger Corneal: Henry Silva; Mrs. Restes: Ilka Chase; Vincent Massler: Buddy Lester; "Curly" Steffans: Richard Benedict; Mrs. Bergdorf: Jean Willes; Peter Rheimer: Norman Fell; Louis Jackson: Clem Harvey; Mr. Kelly: Hank Henry; Young Man: Lew Gallo; Deputy Sheriff: Hoot Gibson; Sheriff Wimmer: Robert Faulk; Shopkeeper: George E. Stone; Miss Allenby: Marjorie Bennett; Orchestra Leader: Red Norvo; Night Club Owner: Donald Barry; Dancers: Laura Cornell and Shiva.

and

Red Skelton
George Raft
Shirley MacLaine

All in a Night's Work (1961)

Director: Joseph Anthony
Producer: Hal B. Wallis
Screenplay: Edmund Beloin, Maurice Richlin and Sidney Sheldon; based on a story by Margit Veszi and a play by Owen Elford.
Photography: Joseph La Shelle
Music: Andre Previn
Art Direction: Hal Pereira and Walter Tyler
Set Decorations: Sam Comer and Arthur Krams
Special Photographic Effects: John P. Fulton
Color Consultant: Richard Mueller
Process Photography: Farciot Edouart
Editors: Warren Low and Howard Smith
Asst. Director: Daniel J. McCauley
Assoc. Producer: Paul Nathan
Costumes: Edith Head
Makeup: Wally Westmore
Hairstyles: Nellie Manley

Sound: Gene Merritt and Charles Grenzbach

Widescreen Technicolor
Running Time: 94 Minutes
Paramount Pictures

CAST

Tony Ryder	Dean Martin
Katie Robbins	Shirley MacLaine
Warren Kingsley, Jr.	Cliff Robertson
Warren Kingsley, Sr.	Charlie Ruggles
Marge Coombs	Norma Crane
Oliver Dunning	Gale Gordon
Sam Weaver	Jerome Cowan
Lasker	Jack Weston
O'Hara	Ian Wolfe
Mrs. Kingsley, Sr.	Mabel Albertson
Miss Schuster	Mary Treen
Carter	Rex Evans
Albright	Roy Gordon
Colonel Ryder	Charles Evans
Baker	Ralph Dumke
Harry Lane	John Hudson
Tony's "friend"	Rosemary Bowe
Customer	Gertrude Astor

Two Loves (1961)

Director: Charles Walters
Producer: Julian Blaustein

186

Screenplay: Ben Maddow; based on the novel *Spinster* by Sylvia Ashton-Warner
Photography: Joseph Ruttenberg
Music: Bronislau Kaper; Conducted by Robert Armbruster
Art Direction: George W. Davis and Urie McCleary
Set Decorations: Henry Grace and Hugh Hunt
Editor: Frederic Steinkamp
Special Effects: Robert R. Hoag and Lee LeBlanc
Color Consultant: Charles K. Hagedon
Recording Supervisor: Franklin Milton
Makeup: William Tuttle
Hairstyles: Mary Keats
Asst. Director: William Shanks

> CinemaScope Metrocolor
> Running Time: 100 Minutes
> Location scenes filmed in Southern California
> Metro-Goldwyn-Mayer Pictures

CAST

Anna Vorontosov	Shirley MacLaine
Paul Lathrope	Laurence Harvey
Abercrombie	Jack Hawkins
Whareparita	Nobu McCarthy
Headmaster Reardon	Ronald Long
Mrs. Cutter	Norah Howard
Rauhuia	Juano Hernandez
Matawhero	Edmund Vargas
Mark Cutter	Neil Woodward
Hinewaka	Lisa Sitjar
Seven	Alan Roberts

My Geisha (1962)

Director: Jack Cardiff
Producer: Steve Parker
Screenplay: Norman Krasna
Photography: Shunichiro Nakao
Second Unit Photography: Stanley Sayer
Music: Franz Waxman, including excerpts from "Madame Butterfly" by Giacomo Puccini
Song: "You Are Sympathy To Me" (music by Franz Waxman)
Lyrics: Hal Davis
Art Direction: Hal Pereira, Arthur Lonergan, and Makoto Kikuchi
Editor: Archie Marshek
Costumes: Edith Head
Sound: Harold Lewis and Charles Grenzbach
Production Manager: Harry Caplan
Asst. Director: Harry Kratz

> Technirama Technicolor
> Running Time: 120 Minutes
> Filmed in Japan
> Paramount Pictures

CAST

Lucy Dell (Yoko Mori)	Shirley MacLaine
Paul Robaix	Yves Montand
Sam Lewis	Edward G. Robinson
Bob Moore	Bob Cummings
Kazumi Ito	Yoko Tani
Kenichi Takata	Tatsuo Saito
Leonard Lewis	Alex Gerry

Shig	Nobuo Chiba
Hisako Amatsu	Ichiro Hayakawa
George	George Furness

The Children's Hour (1962)

Director and Producer: William Wyler
Screenplay: John Michael Hayes; adapted by Lillian Hellman from her play
Photography: Franz F. Planer
Music: Alex North
Art Direction: Fernando Carrere
Set Decorations: Edward G. Boyle
Editor: Robert Swink
Sound: Fred Lau and Don Hall, Jr.
Assoc. Producer: Robert Wyler
Production Manager: Allen K. Wood
Asst. Directors: Robert E. Relyea and Jerome M. Siegel
Asst. to the Producer: Clarence Marks
Costumes: Dorothy Jeakins
Wardrobe: Bert Henrikson, Irene Caine and Ruth Stella
Makeup: Emile La Vigne and Frank McCoy
Hairstyles: Joan St. Oegger

> Running Time: 107 Minutes
> A Mirisch Production
> United Artists Corporation

CAST

Karen Wright	Audrey Hepburn
Martha Dobie	Shirley MacLaine
Dr. Joe Cardin	James Garner
Mrs. Lily Mortar	Miriam Hopkins
Mrs. Amelia Tilford	Fay Bainter
Mary Tilford	Karen Balkin
Rosalie	Veronica Cartwright
Grocery Boy	Jered Barclay

Two For the Seesaw (1962)

Director: Robert Wise
Producer: Walter Mirisch
Screenplay: Isobel Lennart; based on the play by William Gibson
Photography: Ted McCord
Music: Andre Previn
Art Direction: Boris Leven
Set Decorations: Edward G. Boyle
Editor: Stuart Gilmore
Sound: Lambert Day
Costumes: Orry-Kelly
Makeup: Frank Westmore
Hairstyles: Alice Monte
Production Manager: Allen K. Wood
Asst. Director: Jerome M. Siegel

> Panavision
> Running Time: 120 Minutes
> Location scenes filmed in New York City
> Seven Arts Productions

CAST

Jerry Ryan	Robert Mitchum
Gittel Mosca	Shirley MacLaine

Taubman .... Edmon Ryan
Sophie .... Elisabeth Fraser
Oscar .... Eddie Firestone
Mr. Jacoby .... Billy Gray

Irma la Douce (1963)

Director and Producer: Billy Wilder
Screenplay: Billy Wilder and I.A.L. Diamond; based on the play by Alexandre Breffort
Photography: Joseph La Shelle
Music: Andre Previn; based on the original stage music by Marguerite Monnot
Art Direction: Alexander Trauner
Set Decorations: Edward G. Boyle and Maurice Barnathan
Editor: Daniel Mandell
Special Effects: Milton Rice
Sound: Robert Martin
Costumes: Orry-Kelly
Wardrobe: Wes Jeffries
Hairstyles: George Masters and Alice Monte
Makeup: Frank Westmore, Harry Ray and Emile La Vigne
Assoc. Producers; I.A.L. Diamond and Doane Harrison
Production Manager: Allen K. Wood
Asst. Director: Hal Polaire

   Panavision and Technicolor
   Running Time: 149 Minutes
   United Artists Corporation

CAST

Nestor Patou .... Jack Lemmon
Irma la Douce .... Shirley MacLaine
Moustache .... Lou Jacobi
Hippolyte .... Bruce Yarnell
Inspector Lefevre .... Hershel Bernardi
Lolita .... Hope Holiday
Amazon Annie .... Joan Shawlee
Kiki the Cossack .... Grace Lee Whitney
Andre .... Paul Dubov
Concierge .... Howard McNear
Police Sergeant .... Cliff Osmond
JoJo .... Diki Lerner
Casablanca Charlie .... Herb Jones
Zebra Twins .... Ruth and Jane Earl
Suzette Wong .... Tura Santana
Customers .... Lou Krugman, John
                     Alvin and James Brown
Tatooed Sailor .... Bill Bixby
Poule with the Balcony .... Susan Woods
Mimi the MauMau .... Harriette Young
Carmen .... Sheryl Deauville
Officer DuPont .... Billy Beck
Jack .... Jack Sahakian
Man with Samples .... Don Diamond
Gen. Lafayette .... Edgar Barrier
Englishman .... Richard Peel
Prison Guard .... Joe Palma

What a Way to Go! (1964)

Director: J. Lee Thompson
Producer: Arthur P. Jacobs

Screenplay: Betty Comden and Adolph Green; based on a story by Gwen Davis
Songs: "I Think That You and I Should Get Acquainted" and "Musical Extravaganza"
Lyrics: Betty Comden and Adolph Greene
Music: Jule Styne
Choreography: Gene Kelly
Music: Nelson Riddle
Director of Photography: Leon Shamroy, A.S.C.
Art Direction: Jack Martin Smith and Ted Haworth
Set Decoration: Walter M. Scott and Stuart A. Reiss
Special Photographic Effects: L.B. Abbott, A.S.C. and Emil Kosa, Jr.
Unit Production Manager: William Eckhardt
Men's Wardrobe: Moss Mabry
Editor: Marjorie Fowler, A.C.E.
Assistant to Mr. Kelly: Richard Humphrey
Dialogue Coach: Leon Charles
Sound: Bernard Freericks and Elmer Raguse
Asst. Director: Fred R. Simpson
Orchestration: Arthur Morton
Makeup: Ben Nye
Supervising Hair Stylist: Margaret Donovan
Hairstyles for Miss MacLaine: Sydney Guilaroff
Precious Stones: Harry Winston, Inc.
Gloves: Kislav
Miss MacLaine's Gowns: Edith Head

   CinemaScope
   Color by DeLuxe
   Running Time: 111 Minutes
   A J. Lee Thompson Production
   Twentieth Century-Fox Pictures

CAST

Louisa .... Shirley MacLaine
Larry Flint .... Paul Newman
Rod Anderson .... Robert Mitchum
Leonard Crawley .... Dean Martin
Jerry Benson .... Gene Kelly
Dr. Stephanson .... Bob Cummings
Edgar Hopper .... Dick Van Dyke
Painter .... Reginald Gardiner
Mrs. Foster .... Margaret Dumont
Trentino .... Lou Nova
Baroness .... Fifi D'Orsay
Rene .... Maurice Marsac
Agent .... Wally Vernon
Polly .... Jane Wald
Hollywood Lawyer .... Lenny Kent

John Goldfarb, Please Come Home (1964)

Director: J. Lee Thompson
Producer: Steve Parker
Assistant Director: John Flynn
Screenplay: William Peter Blatty
Photography: Leon Shamroy
Editor: William Murphy
Art Direction: Jack Martin Smith and Dale Hennessy
Set Decoration: Walter M. Scott and Stuart Reiss
Music: Johnny Williams
Costumes: Edith Head
Choreography: Paul Godkin
Sound: Carleton W. Faulkner and Elmer Raguse

CinemaScope De Luxe Color
Running Time: 96 Minutes
Twentieth Century-Fox Pictures

CAST

Jenny Ericson . . . . Shirley MacLaine
King Fawz . . . . Peter Ustinov
John Goldfarb . . . . Richard Crenna
Sakalakis . . . . Scott Brady
Miles Whitepaper . . . . Jim Backus
Heinous Overreach . . . . Fred Clark
Deems Sarajevo . . . . Harry Morgan
Mustafa Gus . . . . Wilfrid Hyde White
Prince Ammud . . . . Patrick Adiarte
Samir . . . . .Leon Askin
and

Brinkley: Jerome Cowan; Frobish: Richard Wilson;
Maginot: Richard Deacon; Air Force General: Milton
Frome; Editor of *Strife:* Charles Lane; Pinkerton: Jerome
Orbach.

The Yellow Rolls-Royce (1965)

Director: Anthony Asquith
Producer: Anatole De Grunwald
Screenplay: Terence Rattigan
Musical Score: Riz Ortolani
Director of Photography: Jack Hildyard
Art Direction: Elliott E. Scott and William Kellner
Production Manager: Timothy Burrill
Production Designer: Vincent Korda
Editor: Frank Clarke
Sound: Cyril Swern
Assistant Director: Kip Gowans
Camera Operator: Gerry Fisher
Miss Bergman's Clothes: Castillo of Paris
Miss MacLaine's Clothes: Edith Head
Miss Moreau's Clothes: Pierre Cardin

Panavision and Metrocolor
Running Time: 122 Minutes
An Anatole De Grunwald Production
Metro-Goldwyn-Mayer Pictures

CAST

Mrs. Gerda Millett . . . . .Ingrid Bergman
Marquess of Frinton . . . . Rex Harrison
Mae Jenkins . . . . Shirley MacLaine
Paolo Maltese . . . . George C. Scott
Stefano . . . . Alain Delon
Marchioness of Frinton . . . . .Jeanne Moreau
Davich . . . . Omar Sharif
Hortense Astor . . . . Joyce Grenfell
Joey . . . . .Art Carney
John Fane . . . . Edmund Purdom
Lady St. Simeon . . . . Moira Lister
Duchesse d'Angouleme . . . . .Isa Miranda
Ferguson . . . . .Wally Cox
Norwood . . . . Roland Culver
Harmsworth . . . . .Michael Hordern
His Assistant . . . . Lance Percival
Taylor . . . . .Harold Scott
Bomba . . . . .Riccardo Garrone

Mayor . . . . .Guy Deghy
Mrs. Millett's Chauffeur . . . . .Carlo Groccolo

Gambit (1966)

Director: Ronald Neame
Producer: Leo L. Fuchs
Screenplay: Jack Davies and Alvin Sargent; based on a story
by Sidney Carroll
Photography: Clifford Stine
Music Supervision: Joseph Gershenson
Music: Maurice Jarre
Song: "I'm Gonna Spread My Wings" (sung by Shirley
MacLaine)
Art Direction: Alexander Golitzen and George C. Webb
Set Decorations: John McCarthy and John Austin
Editor: Alma Macrorie
Sound: Waldon O. Watson and Melvin M. Metcalfe, Sr.
Gowns: Jean Louis
Makeup: Bud Westmore
Hairstyles: Sydney Guilaroff
Production Manager: Hal Polaire
Asst. Director: Joseph Kenny

Technicolor
Running Time: 108 Minutes
Universal Pictures

CAST

Nicole Chang . . . . Shirley MacLaine
Harry Dean . . . . .Michael Caine
Ahmad Shahbandar . . . . Herbert Lom
Ram . . . . .Roger C. Carmel
Abdul . . . . .Arnold Moss
Emil Fournier . . . . .John Abbott
Colonel Salim . . . . Richard Angarola
Hotel Clerk .Maurice Marsac

Woman Times Seven (1967)

Director: Vittorio De Sica
Producer: Arthur Cohn
Executive Producer: Joseph E. Levine
Original Screenplay: Cesare Zavattini
Photography: Christian Matras
Music Composed and Conducted by Riz Ortolani
Editors: Teddy Darvas and Victoria Mercanton
Art Direction: Bernard Evein
Set Decorations: Georges Glon
Sound: Pierre Calvet
Costumes: Marcel Escoffier
Hairstyles: Alex Archambault
Makeup: Alberto De Rossi and Georges Bouban
Personal Asst. to Mr. De Sica: Peter Baldwin
Production Manager: Jacques Juranville
Asst. Director: Marc Monnet

Color by Pathe
Running Time: 99 Minutes
Filmed in Paris (Interiors at Boulogne Studios)
Embassy Pictures

CAST

Paulette . . . . Shirley MacLaine

Jean . . . . Peter Sellers
Annette . . . . Elspeth March
Maria Teresa . . . . Shirley MacLaine
Giorgio . . . . .Rossano Brazzi
Jeannine . . . . .Catherine Samie
Second Prostitute . . . . Judith Magre

Linda . . . . Shirley MacLaine
Cenci . . . . Vittorio Gassman
MacCormik . . . . Clinton Greyn

Edith . . . . Shirley MacLaine
Rik . . . . .Lex Barker
Woman in Market . . . . Elsa Martinelli
Dr. Xavier . . . . Robert Morley

Eve . . . . Shirley MacLaine
Henri Minou . . . . Patrick Wymark
Mme. Lisiere . . . . Adrienne Corri

Marie . . . . Shirley MacLaine
Fred . . . . .Alan Arkin

Jeanne . . . . Shirley MacLaine
Handsome Stranger . . . . .Michael Caine
Claudie . . . . Anita Ekberg
Victor . . . . .Philippe Noiret

Sweet Charity (1968)

Directed and Choreographed by Bob Fosse
Producer: Robert Arthur
Screenplay: Peter Stone; based on the musical by Neil Simon (book), Cy Coleman (music), and Dorothy Fields (lyrics) and the screenplay for *Nights of Cabiria* by Federico Fellini, Tullio Pinelli, and Ennio Flaiano
Photography: Robert Surtees
Art Direction: Alexander Golitzen and George C. Webb
Set Decorations: Jack D. Moore
Editor: Stuart Gilmore
Titles: Howard A. Anderson
Sound: Waldon O. Watson, William Russell, Ronald Pierce, and Len Peterson
Costumes: Edith Head
Makeup: Bud Westmore
Hairstyles: Sydney Guilaroff (Miss MacLaine) and Larry Germain
Production Manager: Ernest B. Wehmeyer
Asst. Director: Douglas Green

Technicolor Panavision 70
Running Time: 157 Minutes
Location scenes filmed in New York City
Universal Pictures

CAST

Charity Hope Valentine . . . . Shirley MacLaine
Vittorio Vitale . . . . .Ricardo Montalban
Nickie . . . . .Chita Rivera
Herman . . . . Stubby Kaye
Mr. Nicholsby . . . . Alan Hewitt
Big Daddy . . . . Sammy Davis, Jr.
Oscar Lindquist . . . . .John McMartin
Helene . . . . .Paula Kelly

Ursula . . . . .Barbara Bouchet

and

John Wheeler, John Craig, Dee Carroll, Tom Hatten, Sharon Harvey, Charles Brewer, Richard Angarola, Henry Beckman, Jeff Burton, Ceil Cabot, Alfred Dennis, David Gold, Nolan Leary, Diki Lerner, Buddy Lewis, Joseph Mell, Geraldine O'Brien, Alma Platt, Maudie Prickett, Chet Stratton, Robert Terry, Roger Till, Buddy Hart, Bill Harrison, Suzanne Charny, Bick Goss.

DANCERS, SINGERS AND MODELS
Chelsea Brown, Ray Chabeau, Bryan Da Silva, Lynne Fields, Roy Fitzell, Ellen Halpin, Dick Korthaze, April Nevins, Maris O'Neill, Lee Roy Reams, Sandy Roveta, Charleen Ryan, Juleste Salve, Patrick Spohn, Jerry Trent, Bud Vereen, Bud Vest and Lorene Yarnell. John Frayer, Dom Salinaro, Paul Shipton and Walter Stratton. Larry Billman, Herman Boden, Dick Colacino, Lynn McMurrey, Ted Monson and Ed Robinson. Leon Bing, Sue Linden, Jackie Mitchell and Carroll Roebke. Kathryn Doby, Al Lanti, Gloria Miles, Louise Quick, Victoria Scruton, Tiffni Twitchell, Renata Vaselle and Adele Yoshioka. Chuck Harrod, Charles Lunard, Jerry Mann and Frank Radcliff. Marie Bahruth, Toni Basil, Carol Birner, Donald Bradburn, Lonnie Burr, Cheryl Christiansen, Marguerite De Lain, Jimmy Fields, Ben Gooding, Carlton Johnson, Kirk Kirksey, Lance Le Gault, Trish Mahoney, Walter Painter, Bob Thompson, Jr., Bonnie G. West and Kay York, Leon Alton and Norman Stevens

The Bliss of Mrs. Blossom (1968)

Director: Joseph McGrath
Producer: Josef Shaftel
Screenplay: Alec Coppel and Denis Norden; based on the play by Alec Coppel; from a story by Josef Shaftel
Photography: Geoffrey Unsworth
Music Composed and Conducted by Riz Ortolani
Songs: Riz Ortolani, Norman Newell and Geoffrey Stephens — "I Think I'm Beginning To Fall In Love" (sung by The New Vaudeville Band); "The Way That I Live" (sung by Jack Jones)
Editor: Ralph Sheldon
Production Designer: Assheton Gorton
Art Direction: George Lack and Bill Alexander
Sound: David Hawkins and Laurie Clarkson
Special Sound Effects: Richard Parker
Costumes: Jocelyn Rickards
Makeup: Trevor Crole-Rees
Hairstyles: Bernadette Ibbetson
Production Supervisor: Fred Slark
Asst. Directors: David Bessgrove and Michael Guest

Technicolor
Running Time: 93 Minutes
Location scenes filmed in London, Interiors at Twickenham
Studios, England
Paramount Pictures

CAST

Harriet Blossom . . . . Shirley MacLaine

Robert Blossom . . . . Richard Attenborough
Ambrose Tuttle . . . . .James Booth
Detective Sergeant Dylan . . . . .Freddie Jones
Dylan's Assistant . . . . .William Rushton
Dr. Taylor . . . . Bob Monkhouse
Miss Reece . . . . Patricia Routledge
Judge . . . . .John Bluthal
Doctor . . . . Harry Towb
Mr. Wainwright . . . . Barry Humphries
Robert's Counsel . . . . Michael Segal

and

Sandra Caron, Sheila Staefel, Clive Dunn, Frank Thornton, Geraldine Sherman, Julian Chagrin, John Cleese, Bruce Lacey, Tony Grey, Douglas Grey, Leslie Dwyer, Ronnie Brody, Bob Godfrey, John Mulgrew, Marjorie Gresley, Freddie Earle, Marianne Stone, and Keith Smith

and

The New Vaudeville Band

Two Mules for Sister Sara (1970)

Director: Don Siegel
Producers: Martin Rackin and Carroll Case
Screenplay: Albert Maltz, based on a story by Budd Boelticher
Photography: Gabriel Figueroa
Editor: Robert Shugrue
Art Director: Jose Rodriguez Granada
Second Unit Director: Joe Cavalier
Set Decoration: Pablo Galvan
Music: Ennio Morricone
Dialogue Coach: Leon Charles
Asst. Directors: Joe Cavalier and Manuel Munoz

Panavision and Technicolor
Running Time: 114 Minutes
Universal-Malpaso Pictures

CAST

Sister Sara . . . . Shirley MacLaine
Hogan . . . . Clint Eastwood
Col. Beltran . . . . Manolo Fabregas
General LeClaire . . . . Alberto Morin

and

Armando Silvestre, Jose Chavez, Pedro Galvan, Jose Angel Espinosa, Enrique Lucero, Aurora Munoz, Xavier Marc, Hortensia Santovena, Rosa Furman, Jose Torvay, Margarita Luna, and Javier Masse.

Desperate Characters (1971)

Directed, Produced, and Written by Frank D. Gilroy
Based on the Novel by Paula Fox
Photography: Urs Furrer
Editor: Robert Q. Lovett
Art Direction: Edgar Lansbury
Set Decorations: Herbert F. Mulligan
Sound: John Bolz and Jack Dalton, Jr.

Costumes: Sally Gifft
Co-Producer: Paul Leaf
Production Manager: Mike Haley
Script Supervisor: Roberta Hodes
Asst. Directors: Norman Cohen and Francois Moullin

Color by TVC
Running Time: 88 Minutes
Filmed in New York
An ITC & TDJ Production
Paramount Pictures

CAST

Sophie Bentwood . . . . Shirley MacLaine
Otto Bentwood . . . . .Kenneth Mars
Charlie . . . . Gerald O'Loughlin
Claire . . . . Sada Thompson
Leon . . . . Jack Somack
Mike . . . . Chris Gampel
Flo .Mary Ellen Hokanson
Young Man . . . . Robert Bauer
Young Girl .Carol Kane
Francis Early . . . . Michael Higgins

and

Michael McAloney, Wallace Rooney, Rose Gregorio, Elena Karam, Nick Smith, Robert Delbert, Shanueille Ryder, Gonzalee Ford, Patrick McVey, L.J. Davis.

The Possession of Joel Delaney (1972)

Director: Warris Hussein
Screenplay: Matt Robinson and Grimes Grice; based on the novel by Ramona Stewart.
Photography: Arthur J. Ornitz
Music Composed and Conducted by Joe Raposo
Editor: John Victor Smith
Production Designer: Peter Murton
Art Direction: Philip Rosenberg
Set Decorations: Edward Stewart
Sound: Dick Gramaglia and Gerry Humphreys
Costumes: Frank Thompson
Makeup: Saul Meth
Hairstyles: Ian Forest
Production Supervisor: George Justin
Asst. Directors: Alan Hopkins and Alex Hapsas

Eastman Color
Running Time: 108 Minutes
Filmed on location in New York City
Post-Production at Twickenham Studios (England).
An ITC-Haworth Production
Paramount Pictures

CAST

Norah Benson . . . . Shirley MacLaine
Joel Delaney . . . . Perry King
Justin Lorenz . . . . .Michael Hordern
Peter Benson . . . . .David Elliott
Carrie Benson . . . . .Lisa Kohane
Sherry . . . . Barbara Thentham
Erika Lorenz . . . . .Lovelady Powell
Don Pedro . . . . Edmundo Rivera Alvarez
Mrs. Perez . . . . Teodorina Bello

Ted Benson .... Robert Burr

and

Veronica: Miriam Colon; Young Man at Seance: Ernesto Gonzalez; Mr. Perez: Aukie Herger; Charles: Earl Hyman; Marta Benson: Marita Lindholm; Detective Brady: Peter Turgeon; Brujo at Seance: Paulita Iglesias; James: Stan Watt; Tonio Perez: Jose Fernandez.

The Other Half of the Sky: A China Memoir

Directors: Claudia Weill and Shirley MacLaine
Writer and Producer: Shirley MacLaine
Photography: Claudia Weill
Editor: Aviva Slesin and Claudia Weill
Sound: Cabell Smith
Second Camera: Joan Weidman
Gaffer and Assistant Camera: Nancy Schreiber
Assistant Editor: Suzanne Pettit

16mm color
Running Time: 74 Minutes

WITH

Unita Blackwell, Karine Boutilier, Patricia Branson, Ninibah Crawford, Phillis Kronhounsen, Rosa Marin, and Margaret Whitman.

The Turning Point (1977)

Director: Herbert Ross
Producer: Herbert Ross and Arthur Laurents

Executive Producer: Nora Kaye
Screenplay: Arthur Laurents
Photography: Robert Surtees
Music: John Lanchbery
Editor: William Reynolds
Production Designer: Albert Brenner
Set Decorations: Marvin March
Sound: Ted Soderberg and Jerry Jost
Costumes: Albert Wolsky, Tony Faso, and Jennifer Parsons
Asst. Director: Jack Roe

Deluxe Color
Running Time: 119 Minutes
Twentieth Century-Fox

CAST

Deedee Rodgers............... Shirley MacLaine
Emma Jacklin .... Anne Bancroft
Yuri ....Mikhail Baryshnikov
Emilia Rodgers ....Leslie Browne
Wayne Rodgers................... Tom Skerritt
Adelaide .... Martha Scott
Sevilla ....Antoinette Sibley
Dahkarova .... Alexandra Danilova
Carolyn .... Starr Danias
Carter .... Marshall Thompson
Michael ....James Mitchell
Freddie ....Scott Douglas
Arnold ....Daniel Levans
Peter .... Jurgen Schneider
Rosie ....Anthony Zerbe
Ethan Rodgers .... Phillip Saunders
Janina Rodgers .... Lisa Lucas

American Ballet Theatre

Notes

INTRODUCTION

1. Molly Haskell, *From Reverence to Rape: The Treatment of Women in the Movies* (New York: Holt, Rinehart and Winston, 1973), p. 262.
2. Ibid., p. 243.
3. Shirley MacLaine, *You Can Get There From Here* (New York: W. W. Norton & Company, 1975), pp. 28-29.
4. Ibid., p. 40.

CHAPTER 1

1. Sue Reilly, "Shirley MacLaine Explains," *McCall's*, August 1976, p. 48.
2. Shirley MacLaine, *Don't Fall Off the Mountain* (New York: W.W. Norton & Company, 1970), p. 11.
3. Richard Gehrman, "Shirl," *Sinatra and His Rat Pack* (New York: Belmont Books, 1961), p. 80.
4. L. Stand, "Shirley MacLaine You Never Knew," *Good Housekeeping*, September 1962, p. 146.
5. Rowland Barber, "Hollywood's Most Unconventional Mother," *Redbook*, July 1961, p. 101.
6. Jack Hamilton, "Shirley MacLaine as Sweet Charity," *Look*, July 9, 1968, p. 58.
7. MacLaine, *Don't Fall Off the Mountain*, p. 48.
8. "Mama is a Madcap," *Look*, December 10, 1957, p. 125.
9. "Talk With a Star," *Newsweek*, August 18, 1958, p. 91.
10. Stand, "Shirley MacLaine You Never Knew," p. 137.
11. "Ring-a-Ding Girl," *Time*, June 22, 1959, p. 67.
12. Stand, "Shirley MacLaine You Never Knew," p. 144.
13. "Ring-a-Ding Girl," p. 66.
14. MacLaine, *Don't Fall Off the Mountain*, p. 105.
15. "Ring-a-Ding Girl," title page.
16. Gehrman, "Shirl," p. 78.
17. Reilly, "Shirley Explains," p. 48.
18. Hamilton, "Shirley MacLaine as Sweet Charity," p. 58.
19. Kevin Thomas, *The Los Angeles Times*, June 18, 1968, p. 1.
20. Martha Weinman Lear, "Shirley MacLaine: How to Be 40 and Love It!" *Ladies Home Journal*, March 1975, p. 112.
21. May 7, 1973, p. 13.
22. MacLaine, *Don't Fall Off the Mountain*, p. 218.
23. Reilly, "Shirley Explains," p. 50.
24. Ian Woodward, "Shirley MacLaine, Explorer," *Midwest Magazine*, September 19, 1976, p. 15.
25. "The Diversification of Shirley MacLaine," February 27, 1971, p. 64.
26. John Maynard, "Westward-ha!," *Photoplay*, July 1957, p. 102.
27. Elizabeth Peer, "Shirley's Road Show," *Newsweek*, September 25, 1972, p. 37.
28. William Peter Blatty, *William Peter Blatty on The Exorcist from Novel to Film* (New York: Bantam Books, 1974), p. 25.
29. "In Her Own Words," *People*, May 10, 1976, p. 26.
30. Ibid., p. 28.
31. Ibid., p. 28.
32. Reilly, "Shirley Explains," p. 113.
33. "Good Morning America," June 16, 1976.
34. Julia Cameron, *New York Times*, May 1976, D-1.

CHAPTER 2

1. Shirley MacLaine, *Don't Fall Off the Mountain* (New York: W.W. Norton & Company, 1970), p. 47.
2. Francois Truffaut, *Hitchcock* (New York: Simon and Schuster, 1967), p. 169.
3. MacLaine, *Don't Fall Off the Mountain*, p. 54.
4. Philip T. Hartung, *Commonweal*, November 11, 1955, pp. 142-43.
5. Isabel Quigly, *The Spectator*, May 11, 1956, p. 656.
6. William Whitebait, *The New Statesman and Nation*, May 12, 1956, p. 518.
7. Penelope Houston, *Sight and Sound*, Summer 1956, p. 31.
8. Henry Hart, *Films in Review*, November 1955, p. 465.

CHAPTER 3

1. Shirley MacLaine, *Don't Fall Off the Mountain* (New York: W.W. Norton & Company, 1970), p. 56.

CHAPTER 4

1. Shirley MacLaine, *Don't Fall Off the Mountain* (New York: W.W. Norton & Company, 1970), p. 59.
2. *Around the World in 80 Days* (program booklet), p. 49.
3. Henry Hart, *Films in Review*, November 1956, p. 456.

CHAPTER 6

1. Shirley MacLaine, *Don't Fall Off the Mountain* (New York: W.W. Norton & Company, 1970), p. 92.

2. Bosley Crowther, *New York Times,* May 8, 1958, p. 36.

CHAPTER 7

1. Ellen Fitzpatrick, *Films in Review,* August-September 1958, p. 404.

CHAPTER 8

1. Albert Johnson, "Conversation with Shirley MacLaine," *Dance Magazine,* September 1960, p. 45.
2. Peter Martin, *Peter Martin Calls On . . .* (New York: Simon and Schuster, 1962), p. 283.

CHAPTER 9

1. Holl, *Variety,* May 13, 1959.
2. Penelope Houston, *Sight and Sound,* Summer-Autumn 1959, p. 173.
3. Albert Johnson, "Conversation with Shirley MacLaine," *Dance Magazine,* September 1960, p. 46.

CHAPTER 11

1. Paul V. Beckley, *New York Herald Tribune,* March 10, 1960.
2. Shirley MacLaine, *Don't Fall Off the Mountain,* (New York: W.W. Norton & Company, 1970), p. 114.
3. Ibid., p. 114.

CHAPTER 12

1. Hollis Alpert, *The Saturday Review,* June 11, 1960, p. 24.
2. Marjorie Rosen, *Popcorn Venus: Women, Movies & the American Dream* (New York: Coward, McCann & Geoghegan, 1973), p. 307.
3. Richard Gehrman, "Shirl," *Sinatra and His Rat Pack* (New York: Belmont Books, 1961), p. 83.
4. L. Stand, "Shirley MacLaine You Never Knew," *Good Housekeeping,* September 1962, p. 146.
5. John D. Weaver, "Queen of Kooks," *Holiday,* July 1962, p. 9.

CHAPTER 14

1. Tube, *Variety,* March 22, 1961.

CHAPTER 15

1. Mary T. McGiffert, *Films in Review,* June-July 1961, p. 357.
2. Paul V. Beckley, *New York Herald Tribune,* June 22, 1961.
3. *Time,* May 19, 1961, p. 88.
4. Tube, *Variety,* May 3, 1961.
5. Molly Haskell, *From Reverence to Rape: The Treatment of Women in the Movies* (New York: Holt, Rinehart and Winston, 1973), p. 142.

CHAPTER 16

1. Shirley MacLaine, *Don't Fall Off the Mountain,* (New York: W.W. Norton & Company, 1970), p. 115.
2. Robin Bean, "The Two Faces of Shirley," *Films & Filming,* February 1962, p. 12.
3. Ibid., p. 12.

CHAPTER 17

1. Bosley Crowther, *New York Times,* March 15, 1962, p. 28.
2. Ibid., p. 28.
3. *Time,* February 9, 1962, p. 83.
4. Paul V. Beckley, *New York Herald Tribune,* March 15, 1962.

5. Joan Mellen, *Women and Their Sexuality in the New Film* (New York: Horizon Press, 1973), p. 98.
6. Ibid., p. 74.
7. Ibid., p. 75.
8. Axel Madsen, *William Wyler* (New York: Cowell, 1973), p. 359.
9. John D. Weaver, "Queen of Kooks," *Holiday,* July 1962, p. 9.
10. Robin Bean, "The Two Faces of Shirley," *Films & Filming,* February 1962, p. 12.
11. Ibid., p. 12.

CHAPTER 18

1. Marjorie Rosen, *Popcorn Venus: Women, Movies & the American Dream* (New York: Coward, McCann & Geoghegan, 1973), p. 306.
2. Shirley MacLaine, *Don't Fall Off the Mountain* (New York: W.W. Norton & Company, 1970), p. 115.
3. Rosen, *Popcorn Venus,* p. 307.

CHAPTER 19

1. Shirley MacLaine, *Don't Fall Off the Mountain* (New York: W.W. Norton & Company, 1970), p. 215.
2. Bosley Crowther, *New York Times,* June 6, 1963, p. 39.
3. *Time,* June 21, 1963, p. 92.
4. Judith Crist, *New York Herald Tribune,* June 6, 1963.
5. Crowther, *New York Times,* June 6, 1963, p. 39.
6. Crist, *New York Herald Tribune,* June 6, 1963.
7. Joseph Roddy, "Shirley MacLaine: New-Style Star Tries a Rough Role," *Look,* January 29, 1963, p. 61.
8. Ibid., p. 61.

CHAPTER 20

1. *Time,* May 22, 1964, p. 104.
2. Stanley Kauffmann, *The New Republic,* May 30, 1964, p. 26.
3. Edith Head and Jane Kesner Ardmore, *The Dress Doctor* (Boston: Little, Brown, 1959), p. 140.
4. Patricia Mills, *Films in Review,* June-July 1964, p. 372.

CHAPTER 21

1. Bosley Crowthers, *New York Times,* March 25, 1965, p. 42.
2. Dan Jenkins, "In an Epic New Movie," *Sports Illustrated,* July 20, 1964, p. 52.
3. Ibid., p. 57.

CHAPTER 22

1. Shirley MacLaine, *Don't Fall Off the Mountain* (New York: W.W. Norton & Company, 1970), p. 115.
2. Paul V. Beckley, *New York Herald Tribune,* March 1961.

CHAPTER 23

1. A. H. Weiler, *New York Times,* December 22, 1966, p. 40.
2. Murf, *Variety,* November 11, 1966.
3. Judith Crist, *New York World Journal Tribune,* December 22, 1966.
4. Ibid.

CHAPTER 24

1. *Time,* June 30, 1967, p. 70.
2. Bosley Crowther, *New York Times,* June 28, 1967, p. 38.
3. Ibid., p. 36.
4. Georges Sadoul, *Dictionary of Film Makers* (Berkeley, Calif.: University of California Press, 1972), p. 285.

CHAPTER 25

1. Murf, *Variety,* January 29, 1969.
2. Vincent Canby, *New York Times,* April 2, 1969, p. 38.

3. Andrew Sarris, *The Village Voice*, April 10, 1969.
4. Arthur Knight, *Saturday Review*, March 29, 1969, p. 39.
5. Joseph Gelmis, *Newsday*, April 2, 1969.
6. Charles Champlin, *The Los Angeles Times*, 1969.
7. Joseph Morgenstern, *Newsweek*, February 17, 1969, p. 100.
8. Jack Hamilton, "Shirley MacLaine as Sweet Charity," *Look*, July 9, 1968, p. 33.
9. Ibid., 34.
10. Ibid., p. 32.

CHAPTER 26

1. Andrew Sarris, *The Village Voice*, December 26, 1968.
2. Ibid.

CHAPTER 27

1. Roger Greenspan, *New York Times*, June 25, 1970, p. 55.
2. Stuart M. Kaminsky, *Don Siegel: Director* (New York: Curtis Books, 1974), p. 231.
3. Richard Corliss, *Commonweal*, July 24, 1970, p. 368.
4. Jay Cocks, *Time*, July 13, 1970, p. 72.
5. Kaminsky, *Don Siegel*, p. 228.
6. Axel Madsen, *Billy Wilder* (Bloomington, Ind.: University of Indiana Press, 1969), p. 127.
7. Kaminsky, *Don Siegel*, p. 229.
8. Ibid., 229.
9. Judith M. Kass, "Don Siegel," *The Hollywood Professionals*, vol. 4 (South Brunswick and New York: A. S. Barnes & Co., 1975), p. 143.

CHAPTER 28

1. Penelope Gilliatt, *New Yorker*, September 25, 1971, p. 101.

2. Charles Champlin, *Los Angeles Times*, November 7, 1971.
3. Ibid.
4. Gilliatt, *New Yorker*, p. 101.
5. Roger Ebert, *Chicago Sun-Times*, November 10, 1971.

CHAPTER 29

1. Judith Crist, *New York*, May 22, 1972, p. 72.
2. Arthur Knight, *Saturday Review*, June 17, 1972, p. 78.
3. Andrew Sarris, *The Village Voice*, May 1972.
4. Charles Champlin, *Los Angeles Times*, May 24, 1972.
5. Marjorie Rosen, *Popcorn Venus: Women, Movies & the American Dream* (New York: Coward, McCann & Geoghegan, 1973), p. 254.

CHAPTER 30

1. Author's interview with filmmaker, April 2, 1976.
2. Marjorie Rosen, *Ms.*, July 1975, p. 30.
3. Maureen Orth, *Newsweek*, March 10, 1975, p. 73.
4. Molly Haskell, *The Village Voice*, March 10, 1975, p. 73.
5. Shirley MacLaine, "Back Talk: Propaganda Is What You Don't Agree With," *New York Times*, April 6, 1975, D-1.
6. Shirley MacLaine, *You Can Get There From Here* (New York: W.W. Norton & Company, 1975), p. 183.
7. Ibid., p. 247.

CHAPTER 31

1. Murf, *Variety*, October 19, 1977, p. 25.
2. Andrew Sarris, *The Village Voice*, November 21, 1977, p. 44.
3. Molly Haskell, *New York*, November 21, 1977, p. 89.

Bibliography

"Advance Notice." *Vogue*, September 15, 1959, p. 143.

Alanthal, Rose. "Flying High." *U.S.-Israel Report*, October 28, 1976, p. 78.

Alpert, Hollis. "The Diversification of Shirley MacLaine." *Saturday Review*, February 27, 1971, pp. 43-45, 65.

Baker, John F. "PW Interviews: Shirley MacLaine." *Publishers Weekly*, March 3, 1975, pp. 6-7.

Barber, Rowland. "Hollywood's Most Unconventional Mother." *Redbook*, July 1961, pp. 32-33, 99-105.

Bean, Robin. "The Two Faces of Shirley (interview)." *Films & Filming*, February 1962, pp. 11-12, 47.

Cameron, Julia. "Shirley MacLaine—Back In Her Dancing Shoes." *New York Times*, May 1976, D-1.

Carpo, George. "Free to Have or Free-Love?" *Photoplay*, October 1970, pp. 73, 92-94.

"Cry, Laugh, Cry, Laugh." *Newsweek*, September 5, 1960, pp. 72-73.

Davidson, Muriel. "Shirley MacLaine Sounds Off." *Saturday Evening Post*, November 30, 1963, pp. 30-31.

Dehnsohn, Robert O. "L'Amour Fou." *La Vie*, August-September 1976, p. 8.

"East-West Twain Find a Meeting in MacLaine." *Life*, February 17, 1961, pp. 91-95.

Fleming, Thomas J. "Multimillion Monroe Doctrine." *Cosmopolitan*, July 1955, pp. 58.

"Four For Posterity." *Look*, January 16, 1962, pp. 83-84.

"Fun of Being Look-Alikes." *Life*, February 9, 1959, pp. 12-14.

Garth, David. "Boy Meets Girl." *Seventeen*, January 1964, pp. 79, 101.

Gehrman, Richard. "Shirl." *Sinatra and His Rat Pack* (New York: Belmont Books), 1961, pp. 77-85.

Goodman, Walter. "The False Art of the Propaganda Film." *New York Times*, March 23, 1975, D-1.

Graham, Sheilah. "Shirley MacLaine Fights For Rights." *Citizen News*, April 4, 1970.

Haber, Joyce. "Film Freedom." *Los Angeles Times*, April 12, 1973.

____."He Thinks He's Louis B. Mayer." *Los Angeles Times*, December 4, 1974, Part 4, p. 18.

Hamilton, Jack. "Shirley MacLaine as Sweet Charity." *Look*, July 9, 1968, pp. 56-61.

Haranis, Chrys. "Shirley MacLaine Arrested!" *Photoplay*, February 1965, pp. 21-23, 97.

Harris, Eleanor. "Free Spirit." *Look*, September 15, 1959, pp. 54-57+

Hockstein, Rollie. "Crusades and Capers of Shirley MacLaine." *Good Housekeeping*, June 1969, pp. 52-62.

"I Predict These Will Be the Bright New Stars of 1955." *Look*, January 11, 1955, pp. 17-18.

"In Her Own Words." *People*, May 10, 1976, pp. 25-28.

Jenkins, Dan. "In an Epic Movie, One Dame Beats Another." *Sports Illustrated*, July 20, 1964, pp. 51-60.

Johnson, Albert. "Conversation with Shirley MacLaine." *Dance Magazine*, September 1960, pp. 45-46.

"A Lady in Her Prime." *Show*, May 1971.

Lear, Martha Weinman. "Shirley MacLaine: How To Be 40 and Love It!" *Ladies Home Journal*, March 1975, pp. 28-30, 52, 112-13.

"Lucky Understudy." *Look*, April 19, 1955, p. 90+

MacLaine, Shirley. "Back Talk: Propaganda Is What You Don't Agree With." *New York Times*, April 6, 1975, D-1.

____. *Don't Fall Off The Mountain*. New York: W.W. Norton & Co., 1970.

____. "I Fall off the Mountain." *New York*, December 2, 1974, pp. 63-71.

____. "I Lived With Street Walkers." *Photoplay*, August 1963, pp. 62-66.

____. "My Turn: Shirley MacLaine. Eros and the Nixon

Administration," *Newsweek*, May 7, 1973, p. 13.

_____. "The Pretty American Abroad." *Carte Blanche*, Holiday issue, 1964, pp. 30-31, 37.

_____. *You Can Get There From Here*. New York: W.W. Norton & Co., 1975.

"Mama is a Madcap." *Look*, December 10, 1957, pp. 123-27.

Martin, Peter. "I Call on Shirley MacLaine." *Saturday Evening Post*, April 22, 1961, pp. 26-27.

Maynard, John. "Westward-ha!" *Photoplay*, July 1957, pp. 64, 102-3.

"Miss MacLaine Goes East." *TV Guide*, Sept 25-Oct 1, 1971, pp. 20-22.

"Mr. Parker's Geisha." *Time*, January 27, 1961, p. 51.

Mundy, John. "Sweet, Hot and Sassy." *Photoplay*, December 1955, pp. 56-57, 86-87.

Nichols, Mark. "MacLaine on the Move." *Coronet*, April 1959, p. 10.

Peer, Elizabeth. "Shirley's Road Show." *Newsweek*, September 25, 1972, pp. 36-38.

"Person of Promise." *Films & Filming*, June 1956, p. 18.

Phillips, Dee. "Love Has Shirley Up a Tree." *Photoplay*, October 1958, pp. 4+.

_____. "When Shirley MacLaine Blows a Fuse." *Photoplay*, October 1956, pp. 58-59, 94-95.

"Portrait of a Remarkable Square." *TV Guide*, August 9, 1958, pp. 24

"Redbook Dialogue." *Redbook*, May 1966, pp. 52-53, 99-103.

Reilly, Sue. "Shirley MacLaine Explains." *McCall's*, August 1976, pp. 44-54.

"Ring-a-Ding Girl." *Time*, June 22, 1959, pp. 66-67.

Roddy, Joseph. "New-Style Star Tries a Rough Role." *Look*, January 29, 1963, pp. 61-65.

"Shirley on Way Up." *Life*, March 14, 1955, pp. 102+.

"Shirley's Spoof Party." *Life*, December 7, 1959, pp. 167-169.

Stand, L. "Shirley MacLaine You Never Knew." *Good Housekeeping*, September 1962, pp. 72, 139-49.

"Surprising Spin for Shirley." *Life*, June 21, 1963, pp. 62A+

"Talk with a Star." *Newsweek*, August 18, 1958, p. 91.

Terry, Clifford. "The Happy Hoofer." *Chicago Tribune Magazine*, June 6, 1976, pp. 23-29.

Thomas, Kevin. "Shirley's Quiet Role as an Activist." *Los Angeles Times*, June 18, 1968, part 4, p. 1.

Weaver, John D. "Queen of Kooks." *Holiday*, July 1962, pp. 93-97.

Whitcomb, Jon. "Shirley MacLaine, Sassy and Off-Beat." *Cosmopolitan*, September 1959, pp. 24-27.

Woodward, Ian. "Shirley MacLaine, Explorer." *Midwest Magazine*, September 19, 1976, pp. 12-15.

Index